NOT FOR PROPHET

NOT FOR PROPHET

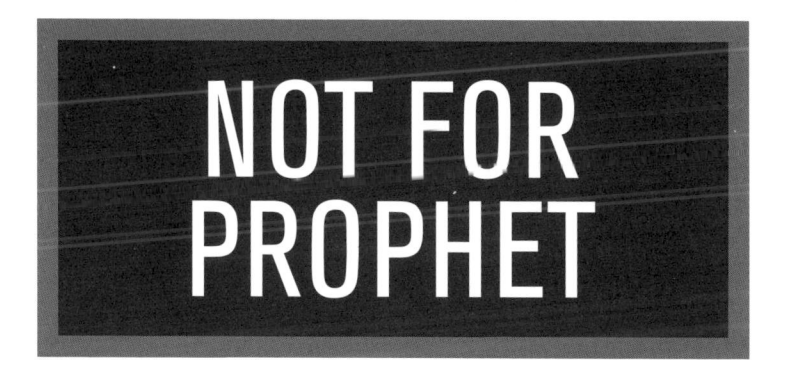

THE ART OF MEN ACTING

BOOK III

❋

Tony Giordano

ANANKE, LTD. New York

Copyright © 2013 by Tony Giordano

All rights reserved. No part of this book may be reproduced in any form without written permission from the publisher.

Cover by: Nicholas Nappi
Editor: Leah Sims

First edition: 2013

Hardcover ISBN: 978-0-9894827-4-5
eBook ISBN: 978-0-9894827-5-2

Printed in the United States of America.

Ananke, Ltd.
% Giordano
13 Circuit Road
Bellport, N.Y. 11713
1 631 803 6013
1 212 947 0443
1 917 592 7212
www.tonygiordano.us
www.brooklynOdyssey.com
tonygiord@aol.com

to

IDEALISTS

ACKNOWLEDGMENTS

THOSE WHO ENCOURAGE YOU TO WRITE BECAUSE THEY ENJOY THE STORIES: JoAnn Tedesco, Michael Mullaney, Ulu Grosbard, Michael Patella, Susan Johann, Jeffrey Hyatt, Joan Valentina, Joan Micklin Silver, Nanjun Li, Theresa Fischer, Joe Sicari, Joe Hindy, Michael Fischetti, Tuck Milligan, Fyvush Finkel.

THOSE WHO ATTEND THE BOOK'S BAPTISM, CONFIRMATION, AND WEDDING: Armand Assante, Mary Joan Negro, Nicholas Nappi.

THOSE WHO READ ONLY THE FINAL DRAFT WITH OBJECTIVITY THAT IS PRICELESS: Karen Whiting, Mark Leib, Guy Gallo, Henry Herx, Peter Morrison.

THE ONE WHO PRODUCES A PUBLIC READING TO LIGHT THE FIRE IN MY BELLY: JoAnn Robertozzi.

HE who provides the Grace.

PREFACE

Family, friends and strangers share lives in the art of men acting.

BOOK I   **BROOKLYN ODYSSEY**
This book encourages everyone to reach for the best that life can offer. Better able we will then be to share humanity. My journey toward self-actualization occurred when I was very young. Despite humble origins, lack of sophistication, no wealth, no power, and no connections, I was able to find my bliss. So I offer my story as a map. Aunt Gracie told me, "Every generation after yours is unaware of how innocent America was, not too long ago, and you should tell them. It may not be too late."

BOOK II   **TONIGHT I WON'T BE ACTING**
After a wonderful life as a freelance theatre director where, thanks to so many productions across America, I had the opportunity to know my country, our society and our corruptions I wrote these anecdotes as examples of the good, the bad, the beautiful, and the ugly to reveal that while I was enjoying my life as a director, our society lost its greatness and both theatre and I became powerless to prevent the loss.

BOOK III   **NOT FOR PROPHET**
This book is written from obscene necessity to expose our faults as we journey on our way to the end of days. My passion was to save the world. But saving the world turned out to be too ridiculous. For, though birth begins our lives, it is hard to cure world woes since we are not present at their creation. Instead we are thrust into life like a suitcase thrown from a fast-moving train. How well we plant our feet on the ground determines how well we can survive. *Not for Prophet* suggests to those who also choose to save this world advance warnings.

CHAPTER ONE

BY THE TIME I WAS FORTY everything I hoped for, and much more, became mine. Like my partnership with Don Linahan, which was filled with support for my career. Like a spectacular career I could never have predicted, again thanks to Don. And like personal leadership that encouraged me to believe I could help create a national theatre.

Unquestionably my first goal, consistent to this day is, I want to live. Don's knowledge of me was usually on target. *"No one faces reality better than you do."* I believe I face reality because I find all that is necessary to live life within life itself. I have no desire to escape woes, so balancing pros and cons excites me.

I was born into a family of real class, known as working-class. *Brooklyn Odyssey* reveals the love that supported the first stage of my journey. This established within me an addiction to expect love and support in all my endeavors. In fact entering a career in theatre promised to be Family, so that is why I entered. My soul became flooded with utopian thoughts. I could actually see utopia as practical solutions to world woes. These ideals never seem unrealistic to me. What does seem unrealistic to me is the mess we presently live in, our commitment to illiteracy, lack of respect for our fellow man, and disinterest in pursuing the origin of our existence. There is at least as much good in the world as there is bad, but if we honestly witness our society today it usually makes us feel there is only bad. Like Don Quixote I know Dulcinea is a tavern whore but within her soul she is also, as Quixote views her, a lady. Such is the eternal argument against those of us who are idealists, that we are blind to reality. While, in fact, we see reality so completely we know it is insufficient to make life work as well as it should, which is why ideals are not the ranting of crazy people. Ideals are answers, but to apply them you have to give a lot, the purpose of this book.

Thanks to winning my battle with my parents to study at Brooklyn

Prep love and support continued to be provided to me by the Jesuits, where they had my back to such a degree they led me into a career I had not even heard of. And assuredly I found love and integrity among the majority of my artistic collaborations, with actors in particular, who sustain the child within. I tried in *Tonight I Won't Be Acting* to avoid talking about how I directed shows. I preferred to let readers enjoy stories of unique performers, in unique situations. So, I permit myself one sentence here to reveal the love of my director's life. *Bringing a play to birth, exploring its soul and its characters, directing actors to become those characters, with designers who most often save my ass, and witnessing what audiences crave and need, especially whenever I am able to provide such for them, is for me Heaven on earth.* Enough said. So be cautious of telling me idealism doesn't work. I am perfecting a left hook for such confrontations.

Because I stood in the center of theatre from sea to shining sea I was forced to recognize the silly reasons why theatre spends so much taxpayer money but creates so little lasting value. As a result I forged a stubborn insistence on justice to defend the faceless taxpayers. The profession of theatre should crave idealism because then the results would reach stars to enlighten a suffering society. But too many bureaucrats control the funds. They have talent only for selling tickets and vacationing in Positano. In addition to them, unfortunately, even most talented artists never dig beyond their talents. Too many of those with a high C assume they created their high C, or high kick, or the gift of birthing productions from zero to opening night with thrilling results. They are talented, some of the best, but they never realize what more would exist if they would explore their talents off the stage and into life itself, caring for truth, justice, family and idealism. It is difficult for my mind to comprehend why so few artists become activists. Instead they want audiences to purchase tickets to applaud their high C. I am not trying to deny the value of ego. We need praise. But so does God. So, say thank you. I just feel that the gift of a high C or any other talent should signal obligation to be grateful to your lucky stars.

Then it is noticeable to me that most of those who acquire the taxpayer money set out to force people they hire to submit to them because their power to hire and fire becomes a weapon. And when they confront someone whom they cannot force into submission they fight behind that person's back, too cowardly for a face to face. Taxpayer money creates as many monsters as the evil marketplace.

And most egregious is that a profession, which should create individuality so artistry can flourish, prefers subjugation of that individuality. Instead of not for profit theatre fulfilling its mandate to create something greater than the commercial theatre it simply used non suspecting taxpayer monies to ape commercial theatre. So many talented people I know were caving in to "Play the game," "Sell out." "Don't buck the system Tony, this is simply the way it is. Give in or you will be destroyed." Of course they were correct, except individuality, freedom and justice to do what is right when you are using taxpayer money demands that you honor your obligation to those taxpayers, or don't take their money and work solely in the commercial marketplace, where those mandates to "Give in or you will be destroyed" are legendary.

I might have been able to accept this nonsense, except I was painfully aware that with each limitation of this kind degrees of fulfillment on stage were whittled away. How can you ask an actor to step up to the plate and create a Hamlet, a King Lear, an Oedipus, a Medea, an Antigone, and especially a Portia if those actors are not able to have powerful, outstanding individuality within themselves? Of course, they can always *act* it, which they do when they *pretend* to be those characters, which is why there is so little genuine connection from the stage to the audience, where the audience can experience truth rather than just become spectators. The drama schools in America will become historically identified as the cause that reduced the beauty of theatrical truth to the fun and games of escapism, while America took a dive. On the other hand so many of our plays reduced themselves to the impotence of life, and this provided opportunities to act without having to reach higher than one's self. One day I was sitting at an outdoor table with a group of character actors when Martin Sheen came by and joined our table. Those who knew him introduced the rest of us, when one of his friends asked, "Marty, what went wrong with *Julius Caesar* at the Public, with Pacino?" and Sheen responded. "I'll tell you what went wrong. That fucking director knew nothing about street people."

I chimed in, "Street people? The most powerful political leaders in history?"

And there it was. If you worked for Joe Papp you were expected to lower every play, unless it was already low enough, supposedly to permit the average person to "Get it."

So during the 1980's my attitude to protect taxpayers led me, step by step, day after day, into the clutches of Scylla and Charybdis, those violently opposing mythological forces. Oddly enough, as an aspect of my idealistic mind, I am grateful to be stuck inside such conflicts because it gives me a perspective I now wish to share with future idealists, one that might provide the ticket to success our theatre deserves, if enough of our artists can put an end to such nonsense. For even as a child I felt with the coming of television and the wonderful PLAYHOUSE 90 and STUDIO ONE, that an error occurred when Madison Avenue stole the power of producing television away from the artists once these advertisers discovered profits from selling soap suds. The artists involved were told to step aside. "Little children should be seen and not heard." Oddly enough, this is basically the same problem I found in Cuba when I worked there twice to direct my musical *Habana Carnaval*, which I will elaborate upon later, except Cuba did not include commercials, just submission.

From my point of view I truly believe that idealism is essential to fulfilling the greatest good of whatever work we are doing. I basically believe such honesty is a sort of religion. From one project to another as we create our shows and provide our communication of life to our audiences we are instigating communications of life. I in no way am referring to established religions because fool that I am I believe theatre is even better if it works the way it should because it provides the fullness of emotions and truth that directly relate to our lives in the here and now. But without idealism, it can't. We presently live in a country divided into tiny categories of people who believe their group is different in all essential ways from every other group. Our theatre fails profoundly to create drama and farce that should have caused clear and undeniable universal connections, white to black, gay to straight, rich to poor. So whenever theatre is just one other attempt to escape from the reality of our lives on this earth it becomes simply one other avoidance of the truth of who we are. This is not the fulfillment of theatre, which should avoid escape, lies, and bullshit at all costs.

There is always a price to pay for one's choices, especially if you want the best seat in the house. What works best for us leads us into some dilemma or another. For instance, I love my childhood, in retrospect, but while I was living it I only wanted to get out. I loved my relationship with Don, but while he was drinking too much I wanted to kill him. I wallowed in my directing career but the more of it I enjoyed the greater became my anger that the industry itself was unwilling to reach its heights, because too many people within it failed to have any vision. The fire that began for me in Prep school was hot as ever and supplied the engine for me to jump from one project to another, from one activist committee to another. But it also created intolerance towards everything because I realized how wonderful my life is, and because I knew I had come from a humble background I felt anyone could accomplish things I was accomplishing but they needed the basics I had been taught. I was my mother's son, realizing that my talent was simply normal, so I developed intolerance for anyone who did not embrace his/her talent. I accepted no excuses when friends drank themselves away from their work, so, of course, I lacked a charitable heart for Don's drinking.

Fortunately Don was a terrific guy and frankly a pleasant drunk, though to me drunk was drunk because it held his talent back. But without the funds to find separate apartments Don and I remained together a while longer. I was forever opening a show and both Don and I loved to cook for large gatherings. Fortunately one of our earliest accomplishments was to improve the terrific apartment we lived in. It was the first floor of a Georgian mansion on 74th street off Central Park, with working fireplace, where we entertained royally, which is why we had no funds.

I restored the paneling in the living room, including beautiful shutters from the early twenties. We hired a short Santo Dominican to paint the room, scrape the wooden floors, and polyurethane. The room became a beautiful site to behold as Don and I worked outside our sliding doors to put wheels on a loveseat while this four foot tall man began the polyurethane. He swished the large mop across the floor. The room was completely empty, except for one tall large pail of polyurethane and one bare bulb from a lamp perched on the floor. It was a serenely pleasant thing to watch until his foot hit the cord that was attached to the electric socket. The lamp flipped over. The bulb broke. The room went up in flames, to the ceiling, from the wet mop, and I became paralyzed. It looked as though this man, engulfed by flames, was starring in a deconstructed production of Joan of Arc. I could not move, think or save his life.

Don, who always surprised me, ran through the burning floor into our kitchen. The man grabbed the large towel hanging from his back pocket, wrapped it around the end of the mop handle, lifted the flaming mop straight out in front of himself and ran out of the building, followed by Don who was running behind him with a ten pound bag of cat litter. I stood in awe, helpless. When the man threw the flaming mop onto the sidewalk, Don ripped open the bag and smothered the flames with litter. I took my first breath at that point, went outside with them, and the three of us sat on the outside steps of the building. Inside the building all the lights had blacked out, smoke filled the interior marble staircase straight up to the top of this mansion, and I took a second, then third breath. We comforted the Santo Dominican and even convinced him to return the next day and start all over.

What was most astonishing is that several years earlier we had dinner guests from California. I don't remember the name of this attractive woman, but I recall her walking to the left side of our gorgeous working fireplace and making an announcement. "I'm a white witch. I think you guys should know that you have a mischievous ghost who hangs around this spot. It is not dangerous, just troublesome." Well, how often does one meet a white witch? And let's be honest, one never believes the first white witch you meet. The only value of even having a mischievous ghost might, I hoped, set such a ghost against our landlady, who was by far God's worst creation, a Puerto Rican bitch lacking every ounce of humanity. Her communications to me always included "Giordano, you son of a bitch." I kept wishing this mischievous ghost would find her way into Inez' solar plexus, but we would have needed a much tougher ghost, probably Medea.

However, by the time our living room was burning we now had new landlords who bragged that they could rid themselves of all tenants because "We are lawyers and know how to lie in court." Once the smoke left our apartment and rose to the top of our building to the apartment of these new landlords I asked Don if he noticed a welcomed peacefulness. He did. Then we noticed that the flaming mop had left a damaged mark in the wood upon the very spot the witch had identified. The ghost with the smoke had left us and rose to the penthouse floor to meet new landlords. So it was no surprise that the husband of our new landlords died three weeks later. He was only fifty-two years old, a lawyer. I believe that he and his ugly wife knew "How to lie in court." But you have to be alive to do that.

How much fun the upper Westside used to be!

At one of our parties on West 74th street a friend who claimed to be a psychic told me my sister was about to snap and "Go over." He told me that he and Theresa had the same horoscopes, and that he also was about to snap; which he did, in fact, two months later. And so did Theresa, several months thereafter, a breakdown that had begun prior to her divorce, which is why I moved her and her four children to my parents' apartment in Brooklyn, and subsequently into a house on Staten Island, the first and only home my mother ever owned. Shortly afterward Theresa regressed into the rebellion she had forfeited during her teenage years.

Life is theatre and theatre is life, both are equally rich in comedy and tragedy. Productions about tits and ass, though enjoyable, are not sufficient to reflect the bleakness in America that was occurring before my very eyes. Weird people on Manhattan's Westside were fighting to kill but their passion extended only to real estate. There was frenzy afoot, and no one seemed to know how to stop it. The world was aflame in financial moneymaking schemes and everyone was behaving as I did over our burning mop, paralyzed. To rescue us we needed a society in search of truth, playwrights mature enough to dramatize universals, and an industry hoping to reach the heavenly stars, not theatre that grovels to sell tickets. But more than anything else we needed to wake up our society to recognize that what they needed, essentially needed, was inspiration to live their lives with more than expensive trinkets.

I worked constantly while my parents suffered Theresa's angers. Of course, I visited, and of course, I called regularly. But for me the pains of Theresa's condition were softened by the pleasures of my directing career. Also, I became passionate that I could, with my well-seasoned grandiosity, wake up my fellow artists, so that we could in turn provide theatre to enlighten our fellow citizens. I became even more active in my dream for a national theatre by embracing committee work on the board of directors at the SSDC and by creating subsidized housing for performing artists who would then stay in theatre to make good things happen. I will not bore the reader with the list of hours spent in committees, only to ask you to trust me when I say it covered a twenty-year period, weekly. But, unlike the problems within my family, which were human and created by life itself, the corruptions I witnessed from my activism were unjustified. While I was struggling to stand up against such corruption the entire upper Westside was purchasing inexpensive apartments and selling them for great profits to buy the next one, and the next. It reminded me of children in Brooklyn who played marbles, and bought and sold new colors from each other.

Instead of purchasing co-ops with the others I grew more passionately in love with theatre's exceptional opportunity to interpret life. I was forever reading new plays and witnessing playwright's views of life, but noticing how rarely these playwrights seemed connected to the issues of our society. Yet whenever I took one of those plays into production I had the good fortune to study characters in the plays and the character of my actors. For me rehearsal periods were glorious. To perfect my directing process for quality rehearsals I used the spirit of cooperation, trust, love and energy I had learned from Brooklyn Prep and my family. My rehearsals were joyful laboratories. The day after opening night I would then investigate how well I had directed and grade myself, as a preparation to better direct the next play.

I was too absorbed to recognize how old I was getting, until my mother pointed out that my hair was turning grey.

"You're too young to become grey."

"What am I supposed to do about that?"

"Dye it."

"Are you kidding?"

"No, they have dyes for men. You should do it."

So I tried. Over a six-month period I used Men for Men since everyone insisted it was simple. Two days of very dark hair, two weeks of almost okay hair, but two weeks of an awful mixture of grey, dark, and dry hair until I decided "I don't have to look at it," and never tried dying my hair again, a symbol of newfound, acceptable reality.

During the 80's my empathy for our society boiled over. It was devastating to predict the destruction of our great nation, but the facts were adding up. I am not a mathematical genius but I always knew that two and two are four because even before I ever went to first grade my father sat me down at the porcelain kitchen table with a pencil and paper and taught me addition and subtraction. Once you discover the truths of arithmetic life follows logically. I identified with Cassandra, the prophetess of doom in Greek plays. For everywhere I turned, except from my family and my past, I discovered people stealing from the taxpayers. It was not difficult to predict that such thievery would destroy our country. But those with their hands in the cookie jar had no conscience to stop themselves, and our government partnered in these crimes rather than monitored such evils. I felt from then on, as I do to this day, that one hundred years from now when students read about the demise of these United States and wonder if any one who was alive at the time was aware that our end was happening I will shout from the grave, "Yes." For, while wallowing in the pleasure from my work, thanks to tremendously talented collaborators and America's wonderful audiences, and while travelling our fabulous geography from one town to another I discovered America's unwillingness to protect the marketplace by refusing to become better people, a sad reality.

My hope for a national theatre became seriously challenged once I fully realized that not-for-profit was actually not for prophet. Plus, Jeanne Dixon's prediction to me at breakfast in the Mayflower Hotel in 1981 "Five years against an army of enemies" was on target. By 1990 I concluded that Americans don't need enlightenment, insisting ever since WWII that all we need is to get laid, get rich, get power. Conflicts within modern plays reveal only whom to blame when you don't get laid, get rich, get power. Why even create not-for-profit when society is capable of paying for entertainments it desires? Take two children to tennis, baseball, or football games, buy each a hot dog, a soda, and park your car. How much? And don't forget cigarettes, beer. Add up underground sums society willingly pays for drugs, gambling, whoring, junk foods and you will recognize how silly it is to ask taxpayers to invest in theatre that is no better than fun and games. We have talents to create shows we like and personal monies to pay for those. A national endowment of the arts (NEA) that was created to do for the suburbs the opposite of Broadway should have created theatre that does not placate but irritates while it entertains and enlightens.

Robert Frost's insistence that "Art must pass through the marketplace to become art," was never obeyed by his friend President John F. Kennedy who helped create the NEA to force theatre upon a public that had little interest in it. Productions that resulted were too often unappealing so audiences were blamed for having no taste. This gave the not-for-profit institutions a chance to beg the NEA and other grant organizations to provide more and more taxes for productions their audiences abhorred. Theaters receiving the grants were not educating audiences, creating companies or developing playwrights. Ironically, they were busy thirsting for hits to Broadway, despite their fake disdain for the commercial theatre. They created no philosophy to justify not for profit taxes. This is a disgrace because theatre can enlighten, as proven by history.

There are exceptions, happily. Adrian Hall and Marion Simon in Providence, Rhode Island knew the importance of creating an acting company and educating an audience. I stood in their lobby prior to eight shows I directed at Trinity Rep, salivating as I witnessed their energized audiences arrive. Marion had reached across Rhode Island to bring audiences to their productions and that made my work joyful. Adrian directed his productions in ways Broadway would never do. He taught his audiences to expect theatre to challenge and be downright upsetting. And he developed a company of fabulous actors. On the other hand, during my time at Yale, I sarcastically asked Lloyd Richards if he knew that black people lived in New Haven. When he said he did, I suggested he invite them to sit among the tweed jackets of Yale's academia in order to create a real audience.

I cannot speak for you, but I need theatre. A truthful play, well performed, makes me more alive two hours later. Theatre helps me witness our human condition faster than the time it takes to live those experiences. Possibly my need for theatre was born when I was young enough not to know better, or possibly things simply were better when I was young enough to see Rex Harrison, Rosemary Harris, Albert Finney, Claudette Colbert, the APA Company, George C. Scott, Barbara Harris, Lawrence Olivier, Maggie Smith, Barbra Streisand, Robert Lindsay, Colleen Dewhurst, to name just a few, in plays by O'Neill, Williams, and Albee.

Broadway maintained high quality throughout the '70's. But not for profit seekers of grants attacked it as inadequate. They were justifying their empty promises to bring theatre across America. During this time Don and our friends enjoyed many a fireplace dinner at our apartment in the days of the Upper Westside after a good show when people were afraid to walk our streets. That was the best time on the Westside because it was never as dangerous as rumored but fear kept the streets empty. The end of this great neighborhood occurred the morning I woke up after flying home from a directing job in Kansas City. Don returned from the store to make breakfast and woke me up with his booming stage voice. "*Haagen-Dazs* is opening on Columbus." A short time afterwards landlords had the courts and Housing, Preservation and Development (HPD) throw tenants out of their apartments. To gentrify, Mayor Koch decided, "No single person earning less than $45,000 per year has any right to live in Manhattan." The middle class sold their suburban homes and moved out of their boring towns and began the co-op boom. While not for profit was extending to the plains, citizens from those plains were arriving for a cosmopolitan life in the Big Apple, dragging suitcases filled with money. Performing artists who had come to New York to write, compose, sing, dance, and act were thrown into the cold like old Indian squaws. Rich kids bought co-ops and completed their scripts in Barbados while poor kids rushed to auditions from the #7 train out of Queens.

Don and I witnessed fat, stupid judges in housing court condemn anyone who fought to stay. Tenants feared reprisals from landlords and the city shut its eyes to atrocities. And the city did this to find a citizenry who could afford expensive condos, theatre tickets, and fancy restaurants, all of New York's upscale improvements. But did these people bring greater creativity to theatre, music, or art? No, they brought taste from forty years of bad television, failed education, money acquired from the real estate boom. In this environment theatre and New

York lost its soul. Las Vegas entertainment replaced the Broadway that had attracted audiences for years, the kind of audiences who knew how theatre enlightens while entertaining, a concept held by Cicero.

Finally Don found an apartment. I stayed behind to fight the idiotic housing court, and I did this while I was trying to correct corruption at Manhattan Plaza, the SSDC, and not-for-profit regional theatre, a huge detour from my plans for a national theatre. This path of my activism caused my enemies to ensnare me within Scylla and Charybdis.

Broadway's show business improved as box office receipts increased. Musicals flourished. And now that we had commercial theatre paid for by rich citizens and not-for-profit theatre paid for by taxpayers we certainly had hope for great things to come. But serious plays struggled to find productions, except great international imports in later years, like *Medea* with Fiona Shaw, *Oedipus Rex* from the Greek National Theatre, and *Waiting for Godot* by the Gate Theatre in Ireland. When theatre is good there is nothing better for, as John Louis Bonn, S.J. said, the audience experiences the entirety of it all at once. Bonn defined theatre as the objective art of men acting. No subjective cameras to block our view.

In its Golden Age Greeks held festivals for theatre and all citizens attended. They shared truths essential to creating a culture, exploring life in tragedy, comedy, farce, poetry, dance, and polemic. Many of their plays reached into the heavens to conquer their gods. Their central character begins as a good man, so that the audience will want to climb aboard his odyssey to experience how close we can come in also beating the gods. But as soon as that character begins to falter from his hubris, we separate from his odyssey to save our ass, replacing our joy for having almost triumphed with a fear of his character for leading us into such trouble and pity for what is about to happen to him. Greek theatre was universal, cultural and spiritual because its sights were levied upon the entire society. Due to the range of topics at the festival, the butcher, the baker, senators, and their families passed through their marketplace during the following year with shared experiences. And look what followed. When has any society stacked up greater art, architecture, music, literature, poetry, philosophy, and drama as was achieved during Greece's Golden Age? Shall we compare? If we had dramatists of the caliber of Aeschylus and Sophocles, we might be enjoying dramas that are indigenous to our daily lives and feel connected to each other.

So, it was argued since the inception of the National Endowment of the Arts (NEA) by those who wrote the grant proposals, if commercial theatre could not achieve such a goal, a not for profit theatre justified taxes by expecting playwrights and directors to dramatize the topics that expose our national psyche. This could have led to universal topics, if they were telling the truth within their proposals for any other reason than to just acquire finances from an unsuspecting public. But most of the deepest issues that do connect us were left out of the equation, replaced primarily by lesser topics that were quaint, but not sufficient to inspire great theatre.

God, for example, is a hot topic. Atheists argue that God must not be mentioned in public places because our constitution demands separation of church and state. Atheists crowd our courts to erase every mention of God. They assume God and church are inseparable and claim that if you mention God you are breaking the law because this insinuates church into state. Where are the playwrights who should be able to grapple with this subject and notice how the atheist looks at the universe, sees a bird fly by, knows every being is born inside females, and says there is no God while the theist watches birds fly by, knows life is created inside females, and finds God. When theists find God or atheists deny God, neither need church. The playing field is equal. So, why is belief that there is no God constitutional but belief in God unconstitutional?

On the other hand, joining a church necessitates membership and therefore obedience to that church's creed, cult, and code. I wonder what Ibsen would be writing if he lived now? It is safe to say that God has existed before church. To be smug about it, God has existed at least as far back as atheists. But I definitely agree that we must keep church and state separate. So whenever someone tries to inject church doctrine into our marketplace that is illegal, because church doctrines are precise rules of behavior many secular citizens choose not to adhere to and that is their right.

I recently argued with a gal who coordinates conferences in hotels where atheists discuss how to take God out of society. To my mind every effort to prevent belief in God is illegal because it is unconstitutional to obstruct religious belief. No one prevents atheists from disbelieving in God. A playwright with the heft of an Aeschylus might write this play. As citizens of the greatest country on earth we should be able to investigate God with the same freedom we use to deny Him. The moment an atheist attempts to stop me in a classroom, or in congress, or on the steps of the White House from revealing my love of God those atheists should be thrown in jail. I even believe we should define meeting places where atheists convene to be their churches and see if they still agree that the very mention to deny the existence of God at those meetings is a conflict of church to state. I offended an atheist recently by asking him to take me to his church one day.

"Church? We have no church."

"Well, how did you come to the conclusion that there is no God?"

"Because I just know that."

"And you did not need any church to teach that to you?"

"Of course not."

"Well, ask yourself why you feel I am breaking the law by believing in God, with or without church."

Venom appeared in his eyes.

Life, its purpose, its origins, our future are metaphysical concerns I ponder and refuse to erase from my brain. If I were an atheist I would still ruminate the universe for these answers. I know many atheists who simply deny the existence of God, like a drumbeat, then refuse any further discussion. Once they make their conclusion, they often tell me, there is nothing more to say. Astonishing! Speaking for myself I want to know more about God whether I am in St. Peter's Basilica or in a bar. It is my right to investigate God, Jesus, Mohammed, Buddha, Krishna, Confucius, Mithras, and Adonis, whomever I like. And I can investigate what their churches say about them as well, without violating separation of church and state, because, I repeat, an investigation of God is not church. Wake up world!

How can we deny our right to enter into metaphysics and search the universe for answers? Can you imagine a world in which Henry Ford did not envision cars? Where would we be without search? Because our constitution gives every citizen the right to freedom of religion you are free to enjoy your findings inside every public institution and if an atheist attempts to stop us, I must repeat, they are breaking the law. You can also apply your religious values to your work, even as President of the United States. The only thing you cannot do, the one that is unlawful, is apply church doctrines to state practices. But your own religious beliefs should not be checked into the cloakrooms at the entrance of state funded public places.

However, I have certain irritations regarding churches. I believe they mislead parishioners in several significant ways. They profess that Jesus suffered to forgive our sins. And they seem to suggest that we need to obey the dictates of their church doctrines before we can reach God. But the bird flying by tells me there is God. I need no other permission. Regarding the crucifixion, in my opinion, God sent His Son to show us that living in this flesh with all of its hellish illnesses will be rewarded. Jesus performs the greatest show on earth. He suffers crucifixion and horror to the nth degree, but only to demonstrate Resurrection, our true gift. He did not come and suffer to erase our sins. Besides, I prefer to pay for my own sins, many of which I enjoyed. I simply point out in my concept of theology that God is love. You go to Him as often as possible and you need no one's permission, which is why we must fight for the right to maintain God in society. And if you choose to join a church, fine.

Once Jesus appeared, Christian churches sprang up and created rules and regulations to honor His teachings. And I believe most churches have been magnificent. They provide sustenance for our heart, mind and soul. In my case I benefitted the way non-aristocratic kids benefitted throughout the Middle Ages when the church would lift a poor kid into education. I love my Catholic background. Church offers us methods to be holy on earth; to deal with our society ethically; and to honor the idea of God, on faith. But churches spend too much time irritating us about our behavior and not enough time helping us to explore the kingdom of God. If we could ruminate God's spiritual world we would improve our behavior because we might recognize that life eternal with Him could give us all that we hunger for. Since believers claim God's spiritual world is superior I always wonder how it works. What does it mean to live eternally as a being in the similitude of light?

So I seek answers outside the church from scientists who might define how the physics and chemistry of light differs from the physics and chemistry of flesh. Faith for me is not sufficient. I want to know, and I do not believe the churches want to take us to that point, despite great scholars, a la Thomas Aquinas, who tried and, of course, Plato, who put one foot forward. I will never stop searching for God, His Kingdom, and His many mansions. And this has nothing to do with church. Of all the good our society provides my religious freedom to search for God is my favorite and America's greatest constitutional gift. Why is theatre afraid of this issue?

I suspect there has never been a more fertile time for dramatists than now. Due to our huge population, the variety of lifestyles, and the imbalance in human supply and demand, there are so many topics to dramatize, if we had fulfilled not-for-profit theatre as we promised. By now we should have dramatized our universality, which Aristotle insisted must come first to create great plays. Instead, most of our plays remain centered upon victims from one group or another where the action within these plays applies solely to the group. In addition, how will our theatre reach the heights of great drama without the conflicts between good and evil that inspired Shakespeare and the Greeks? Secular stories are empathetic but unable to extend universally because in most of their cases the stories they dramatize protect the subjects within these plays by blaming people who did them wrong. In great plays the lead character is both the good guy and the one who makes the wrong decisions that cause his downfall. Modern playwrights leave the audience splinted and as separated after the curtain call as they were before the curtain went up. Our society has created its own Bosnia/Croatia of separate groups all hustling for sympathy and our theatre has dedicated no effort to expose this. During the past fifty years theatre in America chose some form of politics as dutiful subject matter for plays. But politics is a subject that can only comfortably exist within a great Gorky play, for instance, where some one character is the student who rails politically against the system. Drama must extend beyond ideology into universal humanity to reflect the art of men acting.

Another ripe and basic issue for drama, probably farce, is sanctity of the marriage license. Imagine, sanctity bestowed by secular government!

How many evils occur, minute for minute, under this umbrella? Children beaten, raped, locked in closets; spouses destroying each other; troubled youths kicked out of their homes and made to survive the evil streets so their families can pretend to have sanctified marriages? And how sad gays want this license when one of the few gifts for being gay is that you don't have to be straight. This marriage license has become our universal desire. Gays, straights, and atheists want parity from a governmental marriage license. Paradox?

Let us count the crimes in America and then determine what percentage resulted from families who had a marriage license demanding nothing more than a man and a woman, no proof otherwise of any values to future children. After all, to the best of my memory, doesn't everyone come from a man and a woman? Once we attribute sanctity to this license we institutionalize adulation to it. Some people have five, eight, ten marriages in their lifetime. All sanctified? Wow, such magic! Statistics reveal that marriage has failed in its first commitments sixty percent of the time and in re-marriages forty percent of the time, so sanctified marriages are needles in the haystack. Why protect the false definition of "Sanctify of marriage?" Why not define marriage as any ongoing coupling and add sanctified if that marriage proves worthy. Feydeau dramatized how the nouveau riche replaced France's Casanovas and wrote plays that entertained in the process. Who is our Aristophanes, Menander or Feydeau to dramatize the hypocrisy of sanctified marriage licenses?

Young people today engage in oral and anal activity they refuse to define as sex. Girls who want to save their virginity allow anal intercourse, but convince themselves they remain virgins because it was not in their vagina. Language has lost its Epistemological value. If sex can only be vaginal intercourse than gays can never be accused of having sex. Gays might not even have any right to seek a marriage license, which, I believe historically, has depended on consummation of the marriage act for procreation, obviously through vaginal intercourse. As long as gays want a license and since it will not be about procreation, perhaps the gay license should be dubbed a totally different title, to define with reality this separate type of partnership, which is the reality of this issue in any case.

My travels in and out of American communities where I lived for around one month at a time, shopped in their local stores and directed shows for their audiences filled me with firsthand knowledge of how our society was sinking into quicksand. And when I realized that just about everyone around me was afraid to fight just about everything, I became the hound of Heaven. People were not receiving enlightenment from our progressive society. By enlightenment I am not advocating didactics, only the mirror to experience our connection to each other, which is the greatest value drama provides, accompanied with accountability for individual choices.

We have talent to accomplish any goal we embrace because America has a gifted population with all essentials except, apparently love of our humanity and metaphysical concerns. Students, filmmakers, musicians demonstrate brilliance, a sort of show-off genius, but these artists fail to study the human condition to let their brilliance shed light on anything other than their personal dexterity. We built theatres across America, nearly as many as bus stops. We financed playwright conferences and second stages to develop new plays while producing larger plays on main stages. There is no shortage of great actors. In fact, I believe the theatre today survives as well as it does because actors have maintained the innocence of the work. Being blessed for so many years from my collaborations with actors I have reason to love them as I do. Also, designers have provided their special gifts to help directors like myself fulfill our productions.

Playwrights today are not confronting the issues to fulfill universal drama because they have not been embraced sufficiently by the not for profit system nor by the commercial industry to permit them to take the chances difficult choices might require. And no industry can survive without fresh products. Broadway now seems at times little more than bad summer stock, unable even to make chestnuts from days gone by work sufficiently to remount them. And while it is unfair to claim there are no good shows across America it is nevertheless true that too many of them are only expensive imitations of old ones. Playwrights are given one chance to succeed but if their play fails those playwrights are flown over Detroit and dumped into dung heaps. No one in theatre should be limited in that way. Talent takes practice.

CHAPTER TWO

HOW COME WE NEVER MANAGED to create a national theatre? We failed because from the inception of the National Endowment of the Arts funds that were dispersed to create a national theatre were never monitored, and once the funds began to flow they spilled into lakes, rivers and oceans of deceit. And we failed because those who administered the not for profit institutions lacked vision. They convinced their board of directors that they could create theatre in their community but strove instead for personal aggrandizements. "This is all mine" was their mantra. They possessed no motivations different than corporate America. So, they picked plays to satisfy subscribers who had already caused television's dreary death. What they needed has been brilliantly detailed years ago by Harold Clurman in his *New York Times* article for Lincoln Center. They needed Soul. Without soul their vision blurred.

I grew more ferocious in my passion. None of my anger occurred because I was left out of the equations. Quite the contrary! "Tony, come and take over one of these theatres. You'll earn a great deal more than you would from freelancing." I was even offered the opportunities to take over University graduate acting programs. But I decided my contribution would work best if I stretched across borders, worked as much as possible for as many diverse audiences and concentrated in providing services to playwrights, directors and actors so that they could earn a living and stay in theatre. I had the lucky experience of making a living from directing. I felt blessed that I could dedicate my life to theatre. I love theatre but I also love show business, so I have no complaint at either end of the spectrum. I simply want plays that help our society see itself through the great lens of the stage, in its objective reality, my insatiable addiction. There is a farce all around us, and a tragedy in process, but theatre refuses to admit to Cassius' belief, "The fault, dear Brutus, is not in our stars but in our selves." (*Julius Caesar.* I ii)

I chose to travel from one regional theatre to another to instigate the grid for a national theatre, fantasizing that I was travelling in concentric circles with fellow freelancers who sought the same goal. I even enjoyed directing plays that lacked greatness as long as the plays provided a chance for the greatness to occur from performances, so audiences could at least experience quality ensembles and witness actors working perfectly with each other as a metaphor for what people in society should also do. Unlike a poem, a painting, music, a novel, all of which are tremendously valuable, drama is purely about man in action, within himself, in concord or conflict with his fellow men, his God(s) or lack thereof. In fact, great theatre usually follows in any society that has already perfected poetry, philosophy, music, art, dance, architecture and literature because theatre requires a combination of all disciplines.

From the advent of the National Endowment of the Arts (NEA), circa 1964, our promise to provide valuable theatre throughout America began to dry up as quickly as the ink on the first grant proposals. Not for profit theatres further dishonored obligations to taxpayers by incorporating "Enhancement money," undetected by the IRS. This money was a corrupt lie to support commercial productions by pretending it was a gift to not for profit theatres. It was money to aid capitalization of a show on its route to New York, fraudulently permitting not for profit productions to climb on the backs of commercial productions like dogs in heat.

In time I discovered I had no special gifts to change the world except in the space where I was standing, a discovery that took too long to realize. So I transferred my energy from fixing the entire world to at least solving the corruptions that surrounded me. But just bearing witness was not enough. After all, when your country is sinking, announcing that you witnessed the sinking does not a solution make. I fought hard but failed. I present this story now in case one of you wants to pick up where I leave off when I eventually shuffle off my mortal coil. Hopefully, you can find the road to the sun. It exists.

But you must see the whole picture. My odyssey began from humble origins (*"Brooklyn Odyssey"*). But how nice it would be for one of you to begin your odyssey with a panoramic view. My mother was clear. "What do you think, you get off a plane on the other side of the world and everything is better? The world will break your heart. Sit in the corner, close your eyes, and think of nothing. You will go further." Of course she was right. But we are here to live, to fix, to play, to work, to make this a better world. Nothing should cause us not to try, certainly not fear that the world will break our hearts. Frankly, the world has been fantastic to me. I fought for a classical education and received it, worked with terrific people throughout my career, and saw the world clearly for what it is and I am still breathing. I can even brag that now I see good and evil in equal proportions and this vision provides truth. So broken though my heart has been, it is intact nevertheless. And I am grateful that I avoided my mother's fears of my idealism, especially the day she and my father told me, after witnessing my life as a director for about ten years, through its quirky hills and valleys, "Don't ever give up what you are doing?"

Naturally I was stunned.

"What is this about?"

"We have looked at all your cousins, aunts and uncles and realize that you are the happiest."

"Thanks Mom and Dad, I will never give it up."

And I never will. When I directed Chita Rivera at the start of my career she shared her thoughts on this matter. "Tony, regardless of how difficult my life in theatre is I will always love it."

My discovery that not-for-profit was shedding no prophetic light on anything coincided with Jeanne Dixon telling me that I would battle a huge army of enemies across America, and I would be aware of major world events at least twenty years before they occur. During our Mayflower Hotel breakfast her statement horrified me since I was already feeling evil hovering over America. By the early '80s no one believed Robert Frost, nor would they evaluate his prediction that bureaucracy cannot produce art. Instead money was flowing from taxpayers like a summer's drainpipe down the side of a beautiful mountain, but great theatre never sprouted. And Dixon's prophecy that I would wind up in a huge national battle was sad to me, because it meant battling with friends, people I worked with and whom I like. Yes, Dixon was right.

But how unfortunate that such nonsense has to happen. Those battles are unnecessary and based on the elephantine egos of those who are paid heavily in not-for-profit.

Because I function as if I have the testosterone of a pit-bull, I rushed deeper into the fray. In time, as I've mentioned, I discovered that my idealistic intentions merely reveal my dim wit. But this dim wit knows one thing that motivates all of my efforts, which is that our ideals cause us to win a race, play piano, and compose songs. Everyone cheers when grants are awarded to develop new plays, build new theatres, or provide CEO salaries for artistic directors. But within seconds, gluttons swallow the funds and the taxpayers are left in the dark until more money is needed, at which point taxpayers are invited to attend the next fund raising party and served biscotti with white wine.

Evil misuse of public funds adds up to serious corruption. No one person is usually guilty. Lurking behind most corruption is petty greed. People, one by one, simply take something the overall plan does not permit them to have. Someone comes along to condemn the greed. Others hear about this and learn which side is the good, which the bad, and too many then join with the bad, also taking something unintended for them to have. The one who reveals these crimes becomes ostracized and even the people who agree with him go home to hide under the covers.

This was the kind of mess I was in at SSDC, Manhattan Plaza, and the not-for-profit theatres, all three subsidized abundantly by taxpayers. I confronted each group, spoke or wrote, signed my name, sent copies to all parties concerned, including the ones named as source of the troubles, and assumed we would resolve the problems. After all, why wouldn't everyone want to clean up our mess? One reason they wouldn't is because it usually would mean foregoing funds. Another reason is that they would have to confront this issue, boldly, but confrontation is one of the many ugly words our politically correct society has erased. I made many attempts by mailing detailed letters but our politicians refused to reply, despite signed "receipt requested" post office notices, to prove they had received them. And despite the fact that it is their obligation to protect the monies they caused the taxpayers to spend in order to support the legislative programs these politicians promulgated. On one mailing Susan Johann, a neighbor, and I sent forty letters with twenty attached documents of evidence to forty political leaders, including Hillary Clinton and Charles Schumer, to beg them to investigate 169 stolen section 8 contracts at Manhattan Plaza, which was preventing those performing artists from receiving apartments allocated for them. We received answers only from Governor Pataki who at least suggested a different office from his; Spitzer who said it looked as though our concern had merit but his office was too busy so we should find a private attorney; and Virginia Fields, President of the Borough of Manhattan, who told us to fuck off. It is clear to me that our country is full of shit when they announce on TV that all citizens need to do is bring a serious matter to the attention of our representatives and they will resolve the matter. And even when our government actually creates whistleblower laws to protect the whistleblower don't believe it. If you have a serious matter of corruption know in advance you are on your own.

So, after exhausting all other channels, I sent letters to President George W. Bush to resolve the corruptions I was witnessing at the Society of Stage Directors (SSDC) and the Manhattan Plaza's section 8 housing. Somehow President Bush had people who brought him my letters with sufficient reporting for him to tell them to investigate despite his huge international issues. President Bush used his office to investigate my complaints. Yet Hillary and Schumer did not respond in any way, which was astounding in view of the fact that Section 8 housing and the #1 national Labor office were in their jurisdiction.

President Bush was the only one who helped.

Drama and life, each in equal parts of the art of men acting necessitate confrontation, as does leadership, parenting, public office and any other position that requires the ability to deal with corruptions. But I was discovering how impotent our society is to confront truth. And this inability within our society is, for me, the core of our demise. My examples extend to my experiences but locate your own experiences and if you have none you probably have never attempted to resolve any serious matter. Get off your ass and try.

In 1996 I was hired by Boston University for the final day of a PhD degree program in Leadership to put the graduating class through any program I could concoct to test their leadership skills. Fifty well-dressed business people were graduating. I divided them into five separate groups. We spent the day in a large ballroom with huge buffets of food, and large round tables with chairs. So, I gave half of each group a topic and the other half the opposing position. I was working with the assumption that often people feel things belligerently, so leadership requires the ability to unravel heated debates by taking a position.

By early afternoon, however, I stopped the process.

"You all hate what we're doing."

"Yes," they admitted.

"How come none of you challenged me?"

"We didn't want to upset you."

"You just spent four hours doing something you hate on the last day of your PhD program. Does that not justify upsetting me? And not one of you had enough leadership to step forward and challenge me. It is difficult for me to understand why that does not justify upsetting me."

"We see your point."

"Tell me," I said, "What you hate about this?"

"It's too confrontational."

And there it was.

After some further discussion I told them "Leadership requires the willingness to stand up for what is right, not just placate opposing teams. Otherwise you should receive PhD's as Mediators because when fifty people believe in slavery but fifty people do not, making a barbecue might ease tension, but it fails to free slaves who are picking cotton in the fields." Those fifty PhD's now earn high-paying jobs, while slaves, metaphorically speaking, are picking cotton. Wonder why America suffers?

Because of our non-confrontational environment serious plays are losing the essence of great drama, filling our stages instead with one victimized group or another in the spirit of magazine articles. But great plays should have a universal soul. Oedipus Rex dramatizes truth. For instance, how would any of us deal with truth if we condemn whoever causes our plague and then discover that we are the cause? Hopefully the day will arrive when we the people admit we are the cause of our plague. And hopefully a playwright will arrive who dramatizes such a truth. How will we respond? What are our universals, which Aristotle in his *Poetics* insists is the first ingredient for drama? And how can any play have passion and a vision if the playwright is avoiding confrontation? Romeo and Juliet have pure love, which cannot exist in their homes, so Shakespeare lets them take their love through death to a better place, pitting purity against corruption. Lear roams through the storm but discovers the error of his ways and dies once he has faced the truth. In my opinion Lear is not a tragedy because of his discovery. Will we discover our truths before we die, enlightened by our comedy, or die dumb and guilty in tragedy?

But we no longer believe in universality. Each group insists that unless we are one of them, we cannot know their pain. And this limitation of seeing only from your own group's blameless position can never create great theatre. Wouldn't it be valuable for an audience to take a bow, admit the mess we create and discover that we have the power to clean up what we fuck up? Women reject the right of men to discuss abortion so almost all communication is cut off. Everyone is stunned over elementary school massacres and wonder how such terror can happen. The right to kill the unborn through abortion is barely mentioned during these funeral processes, but disrespect for life begins with the right to kill as contraception. It permeates our daily lives subconsciously like mole under the living room rug. Blacks tell us we never suffered in their pigments, so how would we know, thus separating the racial divide as far as possible by refusing to acknowledge our similarities. Gays hide in groups to protect themselves but insult others with open disdain. Only politically correct clichés become acceptable so we can then pretend to be confrontational. *Angels in America* condemned President Reagan for failing to cure aids, while the play's lead character roamed through Central Park having anal and oral sex without recognition of promiscuous responsibility. Political correctness invaded new plays instead of dramas that could unite our universal humanity. It is just possible this foolishness resulted from not for profit taxes that demanded theatre to represent our democracy, through clichés. This problem then polluted plays for the commercial theatre because producers began to shop for not for profit product and give them commercial bling for Broadway.

In the late seventies I asked one of my producers on NBC's *Another World* why our shows around Christmas were more depressing. She told me that Proctor and Gamble took a survey and learned that viewers prefer to watch people suffer worse fates than their own during the holidays. Ponder her answer for a moment.

Years later, when I was directing *One Life To Live* there was an enormous vase filled with beautiful flowers, so I said to the designer who was standing next to me.

"Those flowers look real."

"Tony, they are real".

"How often is this set used in the show?"

"Only today."

"How much do those flowers cost?"

"I don't know. We have an account with a florist. Around four hundred thousand dollars a year."

There is every reason to disdain the commercial industry as well as the not for profit.

CHAPTER THREE

SINCE THEATRE IS FAILING US, let us go to birth where universality requires no playwright. Birth is theatre because each of us is born dramatically so if we could remember birth, it would unite us to every other human being. But we don't. We each began life by living in our mothers, lolling about on her waterbed as we sprouted into our dance of life, then separated from her with at least a ping, if not a pang that should have humbled us forever. How amazing then that birth, this major starring role, is forgotten by everyone!

If only we could at least recall during our births that we chose to kick.

"Let me outta here, goddamn it!"

So we know how to choose. Perhaps it was that act of making our first choice during those intense hours to get out of the womb that instigated fear and impotence because we demanded something that hurt our mothers.

"Oh my God, what have I done? I'm really sorry, Mom, forgive me."

"*Get him the fuck out of me!*"

"Ouch, they're twisting my leg over my head. Some bastard is grabbing my ankles, turning me upside down, and smacking my ass to make me cry and pee in front of my mother no less. Ugh, I'm covered in slime."

We each suffered some form of that trauma but recall none of it. Imagine if we could discuss birth with anyone we met, here and abroad, how unifying it would be. So the first reality in meeting someone would be similarity.

"Did you kick?"

"You bet I did."

Yes, how frightening choice is!

So forever after we manipulate ourselves to believe in our impotence in order to convince ourselves that we have no choice in any matter. And that becomes the only choice we admit we have in common with each other. Impotence!

"I'm only one person, what can I do? In any case, I have no opinion."

"You're right. Our votes won't matter."

"Exactly. No one listens to me anyway."

"I agree. Our lives are not our own."

The power to choose is God's gift for us to be like Him. However, once we admit we have choice, we can no longer be helpless victims, and this would not leave anyone to blame but ourselves. So beginning with birth we choose to hear no evil, see no evil.

If you just glance through classic plays you will notice that they became great plays because they dramatize choice. Notice how powerful man tried to be when he struggled with the gods in those plays and discovered just how far his freedom would take him. Those characters are like drowning men who fight for that last breath of air as opposed to many lead characters in today's plays who lay down with their tails between their legs. "Beat me, because every one already has, and I can do nothing about it. I am no one." I wish I could list the number of new plays I directed at the O'Neill Playwright's Conference in Connecticut where the lead character waited for the play's final minute to declare, "I think I can feel now." I used to tell those playwrights to begin their plays with that line.

When I direct I must find the play's universal principle. It shouldn't matter that I am directing a play about all women, as in *Ladyhouse Blues*; or war, as in *G.R. Point*; or a family opposite to mine, as in *Long Day's Journey into Night*. But nowadays people insist you must be in their category or you are not capable of understanding. It's possible that I know more about black people than some black people, yet there are those who might try to prevent my directing a black play because I'm not black. And so on. It is all too stupid, but it points out that we have fallen into a literal aspect of our human history, one that separates rather than unifies.

Once, after a performance of *Ladyhouse Blues*, I sat a few minutes before visiting my cast while the audience slid out the aisles. Behind me, six middle-aged people, three couples, possibly Jewish, were collecting themselves when one husband asked if the others had enjoyed the performance. All but one said yes. The woman who had not liked it was questioned.

"I don't really know why I didn't like it."

"Well, did you think the actresses did a good job?"

"Yes, they were terrific."

"Could you hear it clearly?"

"Yes, of course."

"So what didn't you like?"

"They made me cry. I don't know why I should cry about Irish women in St. Louis in 1919."

She cried against her will.

I was thrilled.

Knowledge of self should be our prime goal in life. The ideal society would be humanity comprised of individuals. An honest view within our selves would lead to universality because, as the Greeks philosophized, if we know our self we know the world since we are a microcosm of it. I once watched from my hotel room in Italy an Israel surgeon on television say that right before he saved a Jewish man by implanting in him a young Palestinian's heart, "There was a moment in the operating room when I held each heart in my hands, and there was no difference."

Of course, I cried.

That is why we need the artist, playwright, poet, composer, philosopher; those who looked, listened and shared; those who faced themselves and the world they lived in with sufficient scrutiny to notice our joint humanity; those willing to perfect their art to illuminate the truths of men acting.

But if everyone, including artists, want to be #1 and thus superior to everyone else, then all their energies become consumed by competition, which appeals to the marketplace at its lowest common denominator. We then experience little more than artists taunting us to applaud them.

Artists need to rediscover all the voluptuous stages of the human condition and have the courage to dramatize them. Life, death, love, joy, anger, fear, and panic, at root, should be explored. They need to show us that unless we confront our darkest passions and our tragic dimensions, we will never locate our clown. The artist should take us on these journeys. Life thirsts for theatre to replace America's promise of happiness from things. Our consumerism smothered us into believing that profit is everything. Where is the dramatist who knows how wrong this is?

Our dreams cannot be about beating everyone else, mostly because the satisfaction from becoming superior to another person results from false criteria. Outside of sports, where the challenge is against the clock, the other team, the well-placed punch, or the deciding home run, there are no legitimate comparisons. Bjoerling and Caruso may be my favorites, but Pavarotti and Domingo are also my favorites. What is most important is enjoying their talents. Bjoerling makes me see him in action. Caruso satisfies me because I appreciate his bell canto. And Pavarotti stimulates me to go to work and do my job. The great lead us into new places. Keats's "*A Thing of Beauty*" is truly a joy forever. Puccini's romantic passions! Van Gogh's hot yellow *Sunflowers*! Aristotle. Shakespeare. Chekhov. Shaw. Molière. O'Neill. Tennessee Williams. So many gave so much when giving was valued. Yes, the great remember the child within. We should all return to that little kid we left behind as we struggled to toughen up. That child knows our original destiny before we erased it. Take the journey back to rediscover our bliss. I am aware that many scripts have been written to deal with this and up to a point they succeed, but too often they are written with political agendas, not universal vision. Our playwrights might create plays as good as those of our great historical playwrights if we thirsted for that. Or, playwrights might reveal truth anyway, if they know truth.

So, I repeat, since our artists are on sabbatical, we must communicate to each other, boldly speak in an open manner, dirty underwear and all, to become our own prophets. What greater gifts can we give to each other than to reveal our universal natures and share our feelings? Eventually theatre will revive. It always does.

Deep questions begin with children. We must never fear to respond with honest answers.

"Shut up and wait till you're older," is destructive.

When Johnny was three years old, Mary Joan Negro and Norman Snow called from California while they were eating dinner.

"Johnny just asked us a question we feel would best be answered by his godfather."

"What's the question?" I asked.

"I think it best for Johnny to ask you himself."

Johnny is one of those all-American boys who, metaphorically, have Mickey Rooney as their ancestor.

Johnny took the phone.

"Tony, since when I die I go to Heaven, why can't I go into the kitchen, get a knife, and kill myself?"

I simply said, "You can. If you were to die now and go to Heaven, God would love you as we love you. He would be happy to have a three-year-old Johnny to love. But if you stay and live your life, develop a career, a family, then die of natural causes, you will return to God with so much more of Johnny for Him to love."

I paused.

Johnny said nothing.

I had the nerve to ask,

"Johnny do you understand what I just said?"

After a pause he answered.

"Yeah . . . you want to talk to my mom?"

I am happy I did not say he was too young to think such things.

We need to learn to think and reason if we expect to locate truth. Voicing our opinion in any daily poll is not thought. But in order to think we must reveal our feelings and our erratic, erotic and demonic nature. Then we must take whatever chaos and fantasies exist within us and interpret, analyze, evaluate, view all sides of the topic, and come to proper conclusions by investigating with courage and curiosity, not just our own thoughts, obviously, but thoughts and feelings across the globe. We must create true education, not the present institutions that force apprenticeship on students to maintain our failed system of nuts and bolts. Our society fought Russia for years because the Russian system failed to respect individuals, forcing them to become worker ants for Russia. So we fought, and seemingly, won. However, our American society wallows in a system of progress that requires our citizens to survive only when they play the game, give up personal goals, and oil the wheels of our materialistic, industrial society, winding up in the same impotence as Russian citizens. Paradox! Where are the plays to confront this?

We have problems.

The future is dependent upon the past and while the worst of the past must be erased, the best of the past should be savored and brought into the present. This is a difficult task because reality exists in medias res, in the middle of things. Polls have replaced reasoning and communication, but how can any simple answer suffice? We vote yeah or nay, hoping to win in the majority without investigating the topic. As a result we never prepare for real thinking. When thirty-one percent yell, "Kill him," and twenty-nine percent yell, "Don't kill him," we kill him. But who was polled? Morons? In order to think something through, we need to study all sides of the issue. But when does society investigate anything fully? Our society lives and breathes clichés. In our democracy it is time to wake up and understand when dealing with major issues of our humanity that votes in the majority is not always a win. If a majority in our society decides to resurrect slavery we must never forget how wrong such a thing is and be willing to listen to truth even from one person. I believe that anyone who argues that a glass is either half-full or half-empty is denying the fact that the glass is simultaneously half-full and half-empty. Unless you can see that much about the glass, you are not able to discuss that glass. The world is our glass. It contains all good and all evil at the same time. To achieve any success in dealing with life, I suggest we look equally into evil and goodness and use our hearts, minds and souls to sift through the detritus of our society.

Proof that Johnny understood our little theology lesson became evident recently when I flew to LA for his high school concert. It was fourteen years later, an evening of music directed by his superb teacher, Jim Foschia, who in the course of the concert had appropriate compliments that were applicable to each graduating musician. Last among his compliments was his praise for Johnny. "The only thing I can say about John Snow is he is simply the best musician in this school."

Naturally, I cried.

Johnny now has a full scholarship in the Thornton School of Music at the University of Southern California. I am proud to be his godfather. Great youths are available to us. We need to solve corruptions to clear paths for them. It is our job, and frankly, my definition of religion: *making things better for each other*. Mary Joan and Norman are sensational parents. Their elder son, Daniel Snow, just graduated from Georgetown Law School and passed the California Bar exam and Johnny is in demand for stand up bass all over LA. Yes to family, when it is the real thing! "Sanctified marriage" is then appropriate.

As years passed and time approached 2000 I witnessed the end of generosity. Concerned people were replaced with those who cared not a wit to help anyone. During the thousand hours of board meetings I witnessed how those elected are too often unable to rise to the occasion because they lack interest in the general good, interpreting their presence on the board to be an award rather than a service.

"Oh, Tony, we are the board of directors. We can do what we want."

I would read the by-law, "But here is the by-law that proves we cannot do what we want."

Then they would vote, astonishingly, in the majority to do whatever they want, not caring that they are wrong, simply adopting Jack the Ripper's "Catch me if you can."

Troubles never occurred against my work as a director. Had I put all my efforts into production, I would have slid through my career unaware of how many terrible people exist in theatre and government. Had I joined the selfish, I would have reached for the grab bags as they did. Then I would have had to confess, "I am them." And if my awareness of life was limited to knowledge from our present theatre I fear I would be as unimpassioned as those plays. Instead, by entering into so much activism I dipped my hands into the soils of society and saw everything firsthand. I became iron in my resolves. At Manhattan Plaza they closed their eyes to corruption because they desired favors from this convenient cash cow. At the SSDC they seemed hell bent upon power, what little one could amass from such an insignificant union.

So, irony of ironies, being blacklisted forced me to view our world with 20/20 vision. Wherever I tried to help, as I mentioned above, I experienced misuses of not for profit taxes that smelled to high heaven. In time I finally discovered the world evil I had not known during my philosophy oral exam at Fairfield University many years earlier, when I received a 97% grade for explaining evil, with no personal heart and soul behind my answer, no awareness of the insidious day by day corruptions that destroy our programs by people who steal, cheat and lie thus intruding upon every generous program taxpayers are providing, until the funds run dry and everyone looses. In my childhood I was surrounded by peace and innocence, despite a World War, because my family did everything human to make matters better. So, though evil was causing the world to suffer turmoil, I was protected. By the time I stood before those three Jesuits to explain my view of world evil I could only speak out of textbooks, not life. But now as I was discovering corruption in my public life I was attempting to aid my sister in her distress, and guide my family to health.

The corruptions at SSDC and Manhattan Plaza were unnecessary. These corruptions were simply the result of people in power taking what they did not even need. No passion, or human degradation caused them to do this. Just pure unjustified evil. In my family, we faced our challenge openly. Theresa was sick. Her children were growing up in a divorced/nervous breakdown, and her husband refused to care enough to even pay the simple $85.00 per month to help my parents raise his children. But we had no confusion. We dug into ourselves for solutions. My mother was sergeant at arms throughout the ordeal and my father was captain of the ship to stay the course. Progress, while slow, was in sight at all times because we had the will, so we found the way.

To challenge the corrupt tactics of my union and subsidized housing there was no will to improve things, so every attempt at a way was blocked. Instead there was chaos. Language was of no value. Rules, by-laws, promises and decrees to proceed with the subsidy, or the union contracts were vitiated so those who preferred to bypass standards could find a means to agree with each other and avoid truth. By trying to defend the union against artistic directors who were also directors but who refused to pay assessments I studied Labor Law, called THE ACT, and discovered the SSDC was created illegitimately. And therefore the SSDC had no right to use Labor Law monopolies to force directors to join a labor union from its inception. All we had to do to fix this was become a guild and abandon the department of labor's federal protections, providing instead a free right to become a member of a Guild, or not. Within seconds there would then have been no corruption. I brought this idea to my fellow union members, who chose to smother me rather than forfeit SSDC's monopoly for dues and assessments. Isn't life wonderful!

Similarly, at Manhattan Plaza, New York's Board of Estimate Determination to provide Section 8 subsidy for 100% of the apartments was a fantastic achievement, especially in view of the fact that there was no precedent, no model to imitate. To elaborate upon this matter, which I introduced in *Tonight I Won't Be Acting*, once the subsidy was attained, those who stole 169 apartments from the subsidy bonded together: the owners, government (HUD & HPD), tenant's association, and policy committee (unions) systematically altered the subsidy, separating 169 apartments into a fourth category, which they invented to obfuscate the fact that 100 percent of the apartments were assigned Section 8 status. They added a new heading, lying that those 169 apartments came under a separate section, called Mitchell Lama. But those 169 section 8 contracts did, and do still, exist as section 8 contracts. They lied and claimed that only 90% of MP was intended for subsidy. So during the past thirty-five years performing artists have been prevented from living in the subsidized apartments taxpayers provided for them. The crooks rented those apartments to friends, under the guise of Mitchell Lama. Violating the Determination in this manner one simply wonders what then happened to the 169 Section 8 contracts? More later!

The more America legislated, supposedly to help poor people, America progressed into debt, causing our entire country to become smothered within Scylla and Charybdis. Half of our population depends upon government handouts and the other half competitive, greedy free enterprise. We are the house divided and should recall that such a house cannot stand. Citizenship is based on constitutional documents most Americans have never read. And our laws emanate from those documents. It is time to decide whether we want to sustain their principles, whether we need to re-write them, or whether we should return to the corral to shoot it out. The only good choice we should make will occur once we admit the grass is never greener over there, so simply voting for any leader who hates what we have, as do so many Americans, and promises to make it all better, is profoundly stupid.

CHAPTER FOUR

DESPITE SUFFERING FOOLS throughout my activism my directing career filled me with joy. Rarely did day turn to night when I did not thank God for a career that sent me all over the place. It led me in and out of theatres throughout America, Canada, Broadway, off-Broadway, radio, and television. It gave me perspective. In fact my career defines me. When I am directing, sitting on theatrical committees, conferring to discuss improvements in a production, I am a boy scout. I exist for the common good. I don't say this to brag because I am not certain it is a good thing, especially since it exposed the love and passion of my directing career to be my Achilles' heel, which gave my enemies the weapon to hurt me most by blacklisting me from this work. You see, ultimately, Jeanne Dixon's prophesy about the threats against me, nationally, was fulfilled: by SSDC's "labor" union; regional theatres; and Manhattan Plaza's section 8 housing. I thank Jeanne Dixon for her preparing me. She warned me and I did become blacklisted, though there were several productions ahead in regional theatres before this blacklisting was complete. In time I went from having the most contracted jobs per year in regional theatres to none.

At that time a profound aspect of my career ended. "How weary, stale, flat and unprofitable seem to me all the uses of this world? Fie on 't! ah, fie! 'tis an unweeded garden that grows to seed; things rank and gross in nature possess it merely." (*Hamlet* 1.2)

My road to the sun was sinking in quicksand, and none of my collaborators stretched a hand to lift me to solid ground, except God and President George W. Bush. So, personally, I never felt defeated. Stunned perhaps, but never defeated. I see my life as one epic drama, filled with comedy and error but, as long as I remain enlightened, no tragedy. I have always assumed during periods of crossroads I am being sent into some detour meant for me. Whatever doesn't work here works there, wherever "there" is. Good things always exist. My father's words years before supported me: "I never met a man who knows how to take it on the chin better than you do."

Jeanne Dixon's prediction did also, that I would begin to write and like it as much as I like to direct. First I wrote a screenplay, *Brooklyn Odyssey*. Now I have made that screenplay into Part I of the art of men acting trilogy to reveal how family, friends and strangers share humanity. Also, I went to Belgium with Neil Proto for the rights to adapt a Dutch musical about Sacco and Vanzetti composed by Dirk Brosse, we now call *The America Dream*. Then I was asked to write a musical about Cuba. This sent me twice to Cuba, to write and then return to direct it, titled *Habana Carnaval,* in Spanish, which I do not speak. I truly believe nothing can hurt me, other than staying too long at the prom. I should have left the not-for-profit years earlier. Surely I never belonged with people who want you to support their corruptions against taxpayers.

As for God, I often think He has nothing better to do with His eternal time then give me blessings, which began ever since Evelyn and Vincent spawned me into life. Since then I was forever thrown from hills to valleys of emotional trial and error. But each time I was thrown into a valley I wound up on top of a hill.

Finally, as I've mentioned, George W. Bush followed through each thing I asked of him, giving me support by responding directly, and by passing my letters to the proper government agencies. In fact he provided his personal correspondence secretary so my letters were able to reach him directly. President Bush was the only one I found who cared, and this amuses me, considering the view of him from the press and my friends.

When the owners decided to sell the buildings at Manhattan Plaza after thirty years of the subsidy, they did so like thieves in the night, fast and furious, to prevent tenants from having rights. In anticipation of this event, Susan Johann and I took a survey and discovered thirty percent of occupants wanted to negotiate for a condo non-eviction conversion, which would have relieved the taxpayers of further obligations. But the owners, the HPD and HUD government agencies, the MP Tenant's association, and the Policy Committee (eight unions) moved quickly to sell the buildings to Related Co to prevent the success of our survey. To add insult to injury they provided a new obligation for the taxpayers to pay virtually twice as much per month, per apartment. I tried every method known to man to bring this to some legal judgment, but found deaf ears, as I mention above, from Ms. Clinton, Mr. Schumer and thirty-eight other political miscreants elected to protect public funds. I even contacted Steve Ross, owner of Related Co. and warned him that the missing 169 section 8 contracts could one day act as a lien against the purchase, but he obviously didn't care.

I am the glass half-full and half-empty simultaneously; in short, I am the glass. I like to think this is what reality is, combinations of opposing truths. Don Linahan's compliment that "No one faces reality better than you do," is one I cherish. I have very demanding principles regarding the market place. That if you seek taxpayer monies because you promise to do something better than plain ole business, do it, without corruption. Also, it is urgent when you confront corruption that you strike as hard as possible to stop it, even though you will usually fail. Why, for instance, would Manhattan Plaza continue to be subsidized when tenants attempt to stop the subsidy? The answer lies in the simple fact that as long as taxpayers are providing huge sums of money, the crooks can take as much of it as they want. It flows like a mountain stream into direct deposits to their bank accounts.

Where did my idealism come from? There were so many things I learned from witnessing my parents. After all, my mother found a way during WWII, when she was a young wife with two children, no money, no job, and no federal agencies to come to her rescue, to dig down into herself to hold our family together when my father went to war. She was my living symbol of the home of the brave. So when, for instance, I was directing Jo Henderson to be Liz Madden in *Ladyhouse Blues*, I understood, passionately, Liz's anger that the Navy wanted to pay her a death benefit for her son killed in WWI. I can only hypothesize the following, which never happened, but if I ever stole a friend's pen from grammar school, my mother would have confronted me.

"Where did you get that pen?"

And I answered.

"Joan."

My mother would never let that alone.

"Why do you have it?"
"I borrowed it for the test."
"Why do you have it now?"
"I liked it."
"You stole her pen?"
"Yes."

My mother would have walked to the phone, lifted the receiver.

"Call her this minute and tell Joan the truth, or I will."

My mother had no time for nonsense. She was right in your face and taught me to know there is no legitimate way out. Evil is evil and must be dealt with immediately.

And when my father knew that as a father of two he could not be drafted in WWII, he found an honorable method of sneaking into the war anyway by going to the draft board, enlisting, and making it look as if he was drafted. My father had no intentions of hiding from obligations, even while having the perfect excuse. I was thrilled years later to read Pierre Teilhard De Chardin's essay when he was a chaplain on the frontline of WWI and loved the smell of ammunition as men fought for freedom. My father and Teilhard were men of dignity. They "Gave proof through the night that our flag was still there."

My father gave me the following advice when I entered first grade.

"Your mother and I will never be upset with any bad grade as long as you did your best. But we will be very upset if you cheat to bring home a grade that isn't yours."

This caused me to be very relaxed whenever I took tests, and usually such relaxation caused me to do well. Theresa shared these values and, in fact, Theresa had the most-trustworthy character of anyone I ever met. I believe the only difference between us was from her frustration that she was expected to follow in the footsteps of three thousand years of Italian family life, rather than proceed with her fantastic skills as an athlete. And because she never knew how to force her truth to work for her she imploded.

It is difficult to correct our problems, but it is urgent that we try.

We need to view life from every angle because too many issues are causing our house to come crashing upon our heads in the marketplace, schoolrooms, churches, department stores, and movie theatres, all the spots we co-habitat. The poor blame the rich. The rich blame the poor. Both will have wasted the opportunity that is provided to seek proper solutions. Because politicians want votes, manufacturers want sales, and performers want fans, they blow smoke up people's ass by declaring people are always right and they do this so they can manipulate the enormous shopping public into paying for the ridiculous products created by the politician, the manufacturer, and the performer. No one wants to tell people they are wrong, so nothing gets cured. Fortunately some one person occasionally enters history and does fight for truth. Otherwise slavery would still be in existence. Women would have no vote. The gays would have no family except Bloomingdale's. And so on.

We destroy each other every day as if it's a new sport because we refuse to solve problems with clarity. And we lack clarity because we fail to have the willingness to face issues. So we cover our impotence with foolish sentimentality that, "We really care." "We are trying." "Please understand and forgive us." The insensitivity we develop by lying to avoid truths carries over into the insensitivity we feel regarding the number of little children kidnapped, raped, sold into pornography, or murdered, the overwhelming numbers of which should be our wake-up call to the mess of our society. If this did wake us up, truthfully wake us up, we would stop all other activity until this one disgrace was cleansed and children were safe. But we grin and bear it. How courageous of us! Adieu to lost children! Despite all our television programs, films, plays, schools, and politicians, nothing solves this worldwide issue and the reason is because our society simply wants to sensationalize, not cure. But if we cured this international problem, we would develop a unified humanity that could begin the process of working towards other human ills. By refusing to confront evil we let it bloom into three times its original size, like watching the dough rise.

Because Manhattan Plaza (MP) is a great place to live, tenants close their eyes to the corruption against taxpayers, "We deserve it Tony, don't we?" Three former tenants are making a documentary called *The Miracle of 42nd Street*. Their goal is to take the film across America so others can create entitlements of this kind. They debated about shooting pictures of the Olympic-sized pool, five tennis courts, and two basketball courts, fearing to irritate the public during our debt crises. Ah,

Dishonesty, thy stink is everywhere. The filmmakers had trouble deciding what to do with my interview. It contradicts their plan to brag since I name three basic corruptions. I am adamant in believing that if you want to present MP as a model, you must reveal its crimes. Otherwise you are suggesting taxpayers should be duped. Taxpayers should not be asked to contribute further subsidies unless the evils are confessed, so they can at least be avoided in the future. Manhattan Plaza is a great place to live, which is why we created it. But due to the corruptions, the taxpayers are now charged twice as much. Had the tenants bought the complex for condos, taxpayers would have been thanked for the past but relieved from future costs.

I have suggested to the filmmakers that they should become investigative reporters and research my allegations to determine whether I am correct or a crackpot. During the past thirty-five years I openly wrote about this crime to all the guilty parties and always signed my name. It is horrifying to experience their obvious guilt, but when they usually never answer these allegations or only give a "We cannot concur" answer, the evil is exposed all too clearly. If the filmmakers avoid truthful investigation, as they have so far, then they and their documentary should be re-titled *People of the Lie*, to reflect M. Scott Peck's study of evil.

America prides itself on being the land of the free where each citizen can become his or her own person, a land that brags about harvesting individuality. One would have to assume therefore that America has individuals, consciences, and that these individuals add greatness to our country. Yet history will probably record present-day America as the society filled with the greatest degree of conformists, who bend over to support any and every illegal action that benefits them. Admittedly, not all Americans are bad. There is a hefty percentage of true individuals, but either they hide or are so good they can live above all this mess. My conscience would not allow me to hide, for which, I either thank Daniel Berrigan, S.J. for instilling conscience in me, or hate him.

It is sad to journey from our innocence during World War II, which I reflect in *Brooklyn Odyssey*, to today's guilt as I see it in *Not For Prophet*. But I witnessed the evils that abound and I tried to confront them head on. It took enormous effort to battle by myself and loose, but those failures give me the right to mouth off.

How did we make such a mess?

Once WWII ended Americans created every conceivable luxury, personal advantages as infinite as the imagination, and the collective opportunity to forge our own world. Yet today more than fifty percent of the American adult population is virtually illiterate. The marketplace has failed ethics and seduced a market economy where the ends justify the means. Art and education are now mediocre. So-called specialists have no solutions, and pollsters cancel each other out. Explanations are usually materialistic. People who participate in these corruptions often did not create them but witness and remain silent. Or, once they discover whom the guilty are, they join them. Individuality we hoped for has been replaced by the collective need to suck our government's tit, an impossible task with too many tongues thirsting for the same milk.

Money, significant as it is, is not the solution.

Like most Americans, I barely survive our country's pollutants as television unloads its idiocy into my living room. How will we fulfill our American Dream? I guess we must become a third-world country before we admit that we, the people, know or should know deep within our hearts that we create our problems. Thanks to our constitution, we have the incredible opportunity to forge any world we want. We invented every instrument of communication, but we don't know how to communicate unless it's about money, sex, or recipes. When it comes to fixing the ills of our society, we claim powerlessness. We journey to the moon or the bottom of the sea. But whenever issues of morality are brought up, we claim man is never going to change and, worse, that he can do nothing about this. As a society, we simply do not have the will to fix our problems. Yet we waste enormous sums of money to create committees, organizations, foundations, charities, and federal programs to pretend we want the answers to fix our problems, sort of like a patient who lies for years to his psychiatrist to prove that if he fools the psychiatrist he is cured. And our theatre avoids creating characters to dramatize this because it would be politically incorrect to yell to the audience, "Stand up and take a bow for the mess you create". We elect representatives to do things for us we should do for ourselves, and when they fail to fulfill their campaign promise that they'll wash our dishes, we get angry because now our kitchens are so cluttered we cannot cook.

We must try to make life better for ourselves, and for a friend, a relative, a stranger, a bum, et al., by awakening ourselves to truths that improve life and society because whether we like to admit it or not, we are one huge humanity. Health can only occur to a body that has healthy parts. Each family should take care of its members. To tell your child to go to a clinic when you have the money to pay for their teeth is irreligious. When a family cannot provide, then they need money from foundations, education, churches, and social services so leave the money for those in need. There is usually enough, unless money raised to aid the sick and the poor is first stolen by those hired, and paid significantly, to distribute that money. But, once caught, the crooks seem never to pay for their crime. We should make them do so. It is the right confrontational thing to do.

Since drama is the art of men acting, created to witness man in struggle with himself, society, and God, why do our playwrights confront only the truths audiences will applaud? Or do our playwrights only know clichés?

As an example, when I directed Pinter's *The Birthday Party*, I was truly impressed with Pinter's pen. He certainly has the talent to be a great, great dramatist but does he just miss the mark because he may not be enough of a poet to have hope? In *Birthday* Stanley is given absolutely no power to defend himself from two strangers who plan to destroy him. Stanley is a sitting duck, not dissimilar to the daughter in *Night Mother* who tells her mother they need to clean the refrigerator because she is killing herself in ninety minutes, and during those interminable minutes never attempts to change her mind, or be forced to do so by her mother. Then she kills herself. Everyone loved the play. Need I say more? In *Birthday Party* had Stanley fought, whether he won or not, we would have at least boiled our blood in the belief he might win. To hide in fear throughout the play until they erased his face might have given Pinter the facility to dramatize how the totalitarian state of England refuses to permit individuality. But impotency is hardly England's usual thing, at least not since Chaucer. Pinter, they tell me, is a model for David Mamet, and I can see the comparable talents. I directed two separate productions of *Glengarry*, but where was the final act to confront the morality of what happens to these men?

Not long ago pregnant women pronounced that they were not the mothers of the child inside their stomachs.

"But the baby is inside you."

"But I am not the mother."

"Who is?"

"The woman who signed the contract."

Is there no Aristophanes to dramatize such farce?

Sit on a train in the midst of seven to ten black varsity basketball players and enjoy the greatest show on earth, as they call each other nigger for any of twenty different reasons. Then realize this word is no longer permitted and now referred to as the N word, as if it has only one meaning. Society is making taboos of God and the word nigger instead of revealing our obligation to see clearly enough to know that all people in any one group could not possibly be all the same, especially in the worst context. So, I ask foolishly, can no playwright take us on a journey at least equal to a train ride? Artists should look and listen. And speaking personally I am grateful that some Italians are called wops. Otherwise all Italians would be equal. Italians are smart enough to keep the word wop free to be used properly. Michelangelo would be grateful. Tom Sowell is my favorite modern day philosopher, a black man, and I place him on a pedestal.

So, while we await our playwrights I must continue to scream that now is the time for all good men and women to come to the aid of our country and talk to each other, not because any one of us will have the answer, but because none of us has the answer. That leaves a void to be filled by all of us, collectively. Tell our truth, our story, admit what we know, and share it. Ask basic questions. What role do I play in my life? What are my dreams and hopes? How did I betray them? How did I contribute to the national mess? Can I fix it? Do I have the power? Do I have the will? Maybe we might enlighten each other. And for those of us with such high-minded purposes as fixing the world, let us investigate why we failed. This is all about the chicken and the egg. Which comes first, playwrights enlighten audiences? Or audiences have life size questions and seek dramatic answers? Great drama simply presents truth in a fashion no other creation has ever done. It is the ultimate experience of our selves as men in action, when it is not just tits and ass on a stage.

It is impossible to identify the key that caused me to dedicate my life to theatre. Such a thing occurs from numerous episodes in your life. But I believe it was the film, *The Search*. When I was nine I saw it at The Peerless Theatre on Myrtle Avenue by the Fort Greene Project (a cheap, ugly storefront establishment, for $.12). I snuck in one late Saturday afternoon and I did so because I was obligated by the management and my parents to go afternoons for children. So I found one of my devious methods to become an undetected adult, which means I probably just walked through the crowd believing it was no one else's business what I was doing, an attitude that accompanies me daily.

For the next several hours I had the enchilada of experiences. How revealing this film was as I watched with a thousand percent of suspension of disbelief. I was in the film, emotionally, intellectually and psychologically. After all, during WWII no one at home would describe war. My family preferred to avoid such topics. From the living room to the kitchen and back again was our family plan and, of course, with great food. So as soon as this film began, in a flash, hundreds of children, hungry, dirty and frightened spread across the screen and I became one of them. I could feel their hunger. This film brought me into the life of other children. They were alone. They made not a sound. They had no childhood. I had been a brat who had so much to say about everything. But these kids had something taken from them, something so basic. Their fear kept them silent. I was startled.

Next I saw war. Oh, I don't mean battle scenes. I mean war, the shambles of big stone houses and streets paved with clutter. No trees. No grass. No color. Just broken stones. I knew then what bombs had done, and I wept unabashedly over the people inside those destroyed buildings for I could imagine how they must have responded as the bombs were actually blowing them up. I had only experienced the fun of air raid warnings on Avenue U because we had no actual bombs. I learned instantly the difference between playacting WAR versus living WAR. I've never forgotten the difference. It is the default button in all of my work. Then this tremendous young actor, Ivan Jandl, who was my age during the war, ran away from the foster home that was preparing to help him. He was frightened that the American soldiers, because they were in uniforms as the Nazi's had been, wanted to put him back into a concentration camp.

I made a deep comparison with the film, that during the days my family was forcing food down my throat, Ivan was trying to save his life among the rubble of rocks. I tried to think what I would have done. It was difficult for me to come to any answers because these scenes blew my mind and my tears had that awful pain of experiencing terrible moments of life. Ivan's hope for survival occurs when he comes upon Montgomery Clift alone in a jeep eating American cheese on white bread. Clift notices this lost kid and tries to help him. In no waste of time Clift opens his heart, which becomes the soul within this great movie. And what a heart!

The rest is story and plot. Don't let me intrude any further. See it for yourselves. You may not respond as I did, because suspension of disbelief wants to be experienced individually. But that day I learned the importance of story, characters, incidences that make up plot, the universal emotions that wake you higher than a banana split with cherries. My emotions hit the ceiling. Inside I experienced love, empathy and deep awareness, universal principles. For many years this movie encouraged me to study literature, for I admired its story so much. Many years later I became a director, and tried to cause the great things I discovered from this film. Over the years I have seen this film, perhaps four more times. Each time I see it fuller. I learn more. My admiration for the director Fred Zimmerman, Montgomery Cliff, Jandl and the women, Novotno, McMann continues to overwhelm me. It is impossible for me to know how closely what I experienced at 9, or now, is the same. I guess it doesn't matter. For in each case the experiences are great. But I learned from this movie how to communicate aspects of life that an audience doesn't have personally but acquires through this work when artists create such a product. This should always be our goal.

Forty-five years later I sat for an hour and a half on television's *American Theatre Wing* with playwrights and other directors. As usual, the hostess introduced us as if we had just invented gold because only such esteemed people should be on her show. Every question to us was an opportunity to demonstrate our brilliance. Never once did it ever dawn on her to ask us, since we were all successful workers in New York that year, why we had failed to make theatre better. What had we not done? Such boldness is not permitted. But it would have been the truth.

Can we improve?

Our greatness, our strength, our identity is emblazoned upon a true understanding of the American Dream. If that dream has transformed now into nightmare, and we sustain that nightmare at all costs, we will continue to blame everyone except ourselves. What is The American Dream? In an age of relativity I suppose it would be possible to believe there are three hundred million versions of The American Dream. But those are personal dreams. The American Dream is the one that permits everyone the same rights and privileges regardless of race, creed, gender, nationality, and sexual orientation. It is "The" because its umbrella covers everyone. But if three hundred million dreams are interpreted to be "The" American Dream, then we have chaos. If we are to succeed we need to share our thinking, permit others to contradict us, work with each other and forge ahead. Throughout our progressive world we have shaved one part of the constitution after another to satisfy the wheels that screech the loudest, so that by now we hardly know what value the American Dream has for everyone. We need to investigate and study it carefully, and hopefully it will cause us to return to the fullness of our constitution and let it guide us.

Several years ago I was climbing the Santorini cliffs in Greece with a fellow traveller I had only met an hour earlier. As we climbed he kept referring to America's Constitution as the greatest document in the history of man, one that provides for everyone and at the same time has respect for individuality. His name was Nanjun Li. He was about thirty-three years old, born and raised in Beijing. After he made many comments he wondered if he had offended me. He had reason to wonder because my jaw had dropped to my chest for most of his comments. So I told him that he sounded like me; that I was listening to my own thoughts, even in my own words. He was half my age, raised in communism, studying now in Germany but had my words, my phrases, my values. Nanjun is back in Beijing. He just got married. We keep an email friendship. He is one of my favorite people on this earth.

When I taught graduate directors at Yale, I tried to share my ideals. They stared with glazed eyes as if they were stroke victims whenever I spoke of ideals. At the end of the year my directors had completed their graduate productions with me as their mentor so I asked if they had any questions, whether, for instance, any aspect of our year together left anything unsaid. They told me I had left the most important thing out of my teaching. I asked what that was.

"How do we get a job?"

So much for my ideals!

CHAPTER FIVE

BUT OH, POOR TAXPAYERS, once you provide your money, your bucks stop nowhere, no how, nada, mai non mai. Perhaps it is a principle I missed somewhere in my education, that whoever makes the decisions, and/or signs the checks has a royal right to steal as much of those monies he or she chooses. And they cannot be captured, punished, or imprisoned because what they did is not wrong to anyone other than people like myself, and hopefully, you. My idealism expects people with the power over the money to share it properly for the good of the not for profit. And because I hold this position as a permanent emblem of my conscience I become a jerk, in the minds of others. Let me repeat an earlier frame of reference. The greatest idealist of all, Don Quixote, was right. When he looked at Dulcinea she was a lady. When I directed *Man of La Mancha* I never failed to take a deep breath as Quixote sang of his love for this tavern slut who was a lady to him. There is the answer to life in that song.

Through my struggles I was confronting rotten apples that destroy the barrel and because I am not Don Quixote, I failed to have enough vision to have love for these rotten apples. The last time I confronted the group head on was when I was elected at the union to be the lead negotiator for the LORT Minimum Basic Agreement, which lasted nearly twenty-two months. The major issues on my side of negotiations were to deal first with directors who, though members of the SSDC, did not want to pay assessments to the SSDC; and secondly, to increase salaries to keep artists in theatre. I would even fly away from rehearsals to meet in LA, as I did for three full days of negotiations while I was directing at the Dallas Theatre Center.

Talk about dedication!

To what, you ask?

Idiocy, I admit!

I fought hard to convince the opposition that directors were leaving theatre for more cushiony futures in Hollywood. We should, I told them, come to an agreement that would be beneficial for directors to remain in theatre, as well as playwrights, actors and designers. In short I was trying to encourage LORT theatres to realize how essential the artistic collaborators are to the health of their theatres. Can you imagine that such an obvious argument had to be made?

I explained a construction I envisioned to lift salaries. Since each of the regional theatres usually produced six or eight major productions per year in addition to developing other shows in a second space, and since the artistic chiefs for each theatre had negotiated their private salaries with their board of directors based on what they calculated to be essential for them to manage those productions, I suggested we should take the top three salaries from the artistic director, the managing director, and the marketing director, find the mean, then divide that yearly mean into the number of shows each theatre produces. Then we should pay each director this same figure for each show. I further suggested that the lead actors should be granted parity per show, and one playwright per year should be on salary with the possibility for future production. Well, at the other end of the table, they smirked and spewed bullshit.

"Tony, you would be disappointed if you knew how much money we earn."

"I know how much money you earn."

"You think you do."

"I do."

"We earn much less than people assume."

"I've been offered your jobs. I know what they pay."

"Believe us, Tony, if we did what you're suggesting, directors would earn less, not more."

"In that case, you have no complaint. Let's do it."

Their anger at this suggestion revealed the truth.

"Tony, this is foolish. You are negotiating information that is not on this table."

"Well I can fix that."

Then I reached into my folder and pulled out a file from the Theatre

Communication Group (TCG, NYC) titled "Confidential." I lifted my copy for them to see the front of it.

"You all know what this is. Your salaries that are hidden in this document but are obligated to be revealed through the Sunshine Law because they come from the not-for-profit taxpayers."

As they were huffing and puffing and getting ready to blow my head off, I flung the full file across the table and told them to look carefully to know that I knew full well their salaries, and that I had another copy in case they chose to keep that one, though, I told them, "You each have this confidential file. Only the public, the directors, the writers, the actors, and the designers are kept in the dark."

My lily-livered negotiating team sat next to me, frightened. Later they asked, "How could you fight so hard? They'll never forgive you."

"You elected me, did you not?"

"Yes, but, Tony, you'll never work for them again."

And, of course, I didn't.

Weeks later, Peter Zeisler, the head of the Theatre Communication Group (TCG) attacked me for revealing his precious "Confidential" file. Can you imagine this idiot had no conscience to realize that he was heading a not-for-profit organization to help artists communicate with each other, but was hiding essential information? Worse yet, Peter actually said,

"Tony, did you not notice the file was called Confidential"?

"Had I known years ago you were hiding this information, I would have exposed it then."

And of course he never spoke to me afterward. By now the list of my enemies was growing daily. In time I have learned to be grateful so I can see them coming.

Imagine typing "Confidential," then assuming I was obligated to keep his secret?

Across the negotiating table the LORT negotiating team had the power to negotiate such a salary possibility but chose to destroy the opportunity, preferring instead to screech because I had revealed their salaries. That is too often how we proceed. No discussion of new possibilities, no investigation, no evaluations. No belief in the possibility that they should look anew, listen to anything that might improve not for profit theatres. Instead they reveal the innate farce they instigate because of their greed. And that is why things remain unimproved. When I was a boy in Brooklyn we played tag. Once tagged you were caught. Menander, the Greek playwright, could weave a play around that LORT negotiation.

The refusal of artistic directors to pay assessments continued. So within one week I flew to five meetings in five cities from New York to LA asking the membership who attended those meetings, including the very artistic directors attending who refused to pay assessments, to vote whether they would strike if this matter could not be resolved. Votes were gathered by hand and totaled in favor of a strike. The SSDC contract went nationally before the Membership to be ratified with the proviso that every director, for every production, was obligated to pay assessments. "One for all, all for one" would continue to be SSDC's motto. We kept the entire membership properly informed. The contract was ratified. Clearly, the twenty-two months of negotiation ended triumphantly. I then accepted five directing jobs to immerse myself back into my work.

Mendacity pervaded all of our programs. And because there is a transfer of learning, which involves the ability to transfer one learning experience to another wherever I smelled trouble I refused to walk away. I noticed that every time we suffer a mass killing, especially in one of our innocent elementary schools, but obviously I extend this to any massacre, our TV's broadcast, "How can such a thing happen to these innocent children, in this wonderful village?" Then the politicos arrive. "Guns must be more difficult to purchase. God does not care. Schools need to hire police to guard the children. Principals should carry guns." I do not mean to insult those answers except to point out that none of those answers conquer the issue because the majority of people who argue for those solutions support abortion, love Hollywood's gun-for-the-fun-of it movies, and manufacture games for kids to experience killing on their home screens to get a good taste of massacre. They refuse to study abortions and how they destroy not just one particular life, but infest a social disrespect for all life. I recognize this is the law of the land but that should not stop us from measuring what even legal abortions costs us in society on the days we are crying for our massacred children. After all, lack of respect for life is lack of respect for life. Films that wallow in gunfights for entertainment might have more to do with the problem of massacres than the purchase of guns. Take guns away, but keep abortion and movie gun fights, knives will wind up as the weapons, or sticks and stones. Once the right to kill the innocent permeates the citizenry the taste for blood is established.

CHAPTER SIX

DURING THE NEXT FIVE MONTHS, I directed *A Quiet End,* a play by Robin Swados about three guys with AIDS who share an apartment. I also directed a production of *Lend Me a Tenor* at Trinity Rep, which was acclaimed by the Boston critics to be the best ensemble production in Trinity's history, so Trinity asked me to come back with a second cast and extend the run, which I did. I was writing my screenplay of *Brooklyn Odyssey* around four fifteen a.m. I directed *Harvest,* a half hour video for cable television produced by Trinity Church, about a murdered young man in Texas whose young wife agreed to have his organs harvested, but one year later wants to meet the man so she can listen to the heart. She finds a way to do this. And I was directing ABC's *Loving* in NYC.

In *A Quiet End* I directed Lonny Price, Jordan Mott, Rob Gomes, Phillip Coccioletti and Paul Millikin. The rehearsals were very moving and the play, though good, suffered from being produced five years too late. And with Lonny Price in the lead, rehearsals were enriched because Lonny can act and so could the other actors. Every time I directed a particular scene in act 2 where Jordan Mott's character, Billy, explained to Lonny's character, Max, that he was moving because he wanted his family on the farm in Idaho to know he was gay and to die surrounded by his loved ones where he could play his old piano, I would cry. The scene was wonderfully written by Robin, and brilliantly performed by Jordan Mott and Lonny. I cried every time.

On opening night when John Simon arrived to review the show I bet one of the producers he would not remain for the second act because act 1 ended with a kiss of intense passion during which Rob Gomes attempts to prove to Lonny that he is not breaking up with him for fear of contamination but because he fell out of love. We rehearsed that kiss until it was dangerous in every way. John Simon left the theatre and walked off, turning the corner out of sight. I won the bet, I assumed. But as the lights were about to dim, John Simon returned and sat again two seats in front of me. When Jordan told Lonny he was returning to Idaho, John Simon wept in the exact spot I always wept and wiped his face and nose thereafter. His review bragged for two paragraphs that Jordan Mott gave the most sensitive performance he had ever seen from a young actor.

When I met Simon at a dinner party thrown by Nancy and Phil Bosco several years later, I told this story to the table of guests. "We think of John as homophobic, but let me tell you. . . ."

As soon as I finished telling the story, Simon simply nodded his head and asked, "How is Jordan?"

I explained, "Your incredible review should have pushed him into constant acclaim. But one year later when he and his girlfriend came to my apartment for dinner, Jordan told me he had not had one audition in the entire year." No amazing grace in this industry.

❉

I FIRST REFUSED TO DIRECT *Lend Me a Tenor*, because I saw the Broadway production and usually never direct anything I've seen. But Trinity could always seduce me. "We lost our subscribers, and if you direct this we'll get them back." One would think I was above such flattery, but frankly, just blow the smoke and I'll follow you anywhere. So I told them to send me a copy and I would read it and make a decision. The play read quite differently from what I had seen on Broadway, so I realized my argument was with the production.

At Trinity, I explained to the cast that the play is farcical mostly because it dramatizes different realities from the ones in the characters fantasies. As one example, the tenor has a glass of wine so they believe he is an alcoholic. But, simply put, he is Italian and this is a glass of wine. There is no reason the tenor should play it as an alcoholic. In fact it is necessary that he be a warm, caring man because of the help he shows the young American singer. In a Feydeau farce the character that borrows his neighbor's wife for a fling in a hotel proves unable to fulfill his dream because Feydeau was revealing the impotence that became France once the nouveau rich replaced the cavalier. In *Tenor* everyone is innocent, just a local amateur opera company. Well, *Tenor* at Trinity was superb, the cast as usual at Trinity Rep sensational, the humanity fabulous, and the farce, funnier than one could ever hope for.

❋

Harvest required cutting the script from one hour to a half hour, though I believe the story suffered from being shortened. However, I enjoyed making this little film. The author, Richard Selzer found this real story about this Texas couple and did a nice job of writing it. But he wanted a hot young actor to play the man who receives the heart, and I cast a talented actor of middle age. I had no idea until after I shot the film that Selzer would complain that when the guy took off his shirt to allow the dead man's wife to listen to her husband's heart Selzer expected him to be sexy. *Harvest* had fantastic actors and worked well.

❋

JACKIE BABBIN CALLED TO TELL ME she was now the producer of *Loving*, an ABC soap opera. Would I come and direct it? I told her I hated soaps, and I hadn't directed one in twelve years. I didn't know how anymore. Jackie said that wasn't possible. I insisted it was. Then that smoke began, "This show needs your energy. These actors are deadly, Tony, please come and help us." It never fails. I should rent out as a black belly stove.

So I sauntered over to ABC's studio, received the script, met the staff, checked out the sets, and went home. What did I find? The script included three scenes in a House of Mirrors. A young woman is caught inside these mirrors and is hounded by a man who wants to kill her. The next day I called the designer.

"Have you ever used this set?"

"No."

"Will it be used subsequently or previously?"

"No."

"Do you know how to shoot inside this set?"

"No."

"Me neither."
"You'll figure it out."
"Have you designed it yet?"
"No."
"How soon will you?"
"The day before you shoot the scene."
"I don't know how to shoot this scene."
"You'll figure it out."
"I don't think so."
"Sure you will. You'll see."

So, the awful day arrived. I had told the truth, but no one believed me. In daytime soap there is an acceptance that you never say you don't know how to do something. No one ever knows how to do it, whatever the "it" is, so as long as you do something, the others applaud as if that is how the "it" was supposed to be done. Everyone is faking, which is why it always comes off as crap.

I shot all the other scenes first, and Jackie was thrilled. "Wow, what energy. We've never seen these actors this awake before. They're talking to each other with passion. Tony, you are fabulous."

"Jackie, hold your praise for the mirror scenes."

Then mayhem! No matter where I placed the actors and the cameras, the mirrors revealed everything. There were no secret places. I needed different dialogue, "Oh hi, good, you're here. I think I'll kill you now."

So I asked the technical staff in the booth if they were able to forget the shots I'd written in the master script and simply follow my calls. They said yes. I announced I would go on the set and give the actors and the cameras new positions, and then I would return and wing it. And so I did. Surprisingly, I was able to look into the extra monitors as the actors spoke and wherever I did not see a camera in a mirror, and I could see only one actor at a time, I took that shot, and did the same, again and again until I finished three scenes in that way.

Jackie called me next day at six a.m. and told me she had never seen such improvisational spontaneity and asked if I would come and direct every week. "Never seen such spontaneity" was sufficient smoke to fool me once again. Works every time! How odd to be such a jerk, for a man who pretends to have a principled life!

I continued to write *Brooklyn Odyssey*, which I did for five months in the middle of the night. It was my special new gift, to wake without any alarm clock at 4:15 am, make a pot of coffee, and write film scenes. God was at it again!

CHAPTER SEVEN

WHEN THE CATS AWAY, the mice will play.

While I was catching up on my career, the entire twenty-two months of properly executed negotiations were corrupted beyond belief by idiots at the SSDC who wanted the contract to be the opposite from what the Membership ratified, so they proceeded to meet, in secret, with artistic directors and their lawyer, to corrupt all the union's legitimate negotiation of this contract. They created *The Memorandum of Understanding*, giving to Artistic Directors, when they directed a play in their theatres, the perpetual right to pay no assessments, remain in good standing, and be members of the Board of Directors at the SSDC to decide on all policies for all directors. I only wish I am lying.

This memorandum undid every aspect of the so-called brotherhood and the entire concept of labor law negotiations. It was the ultimate labor union corruption. The membership were given no opportunity to either ratify or vote on this memorandum, except for a meeting in a virtual kangaroo court, which bypassed the entire membership's negotiating processes. What should be the name of their outrageous behavior? Did they even have enough conscience to care what they did? Obviously not! Has anyone within the union these past fifteen years resolved this problem? No.

My suspicion as to why these disgruntled artistic directors wanted special treatment was not only because they resented the measly two hundred dollars in assessments they would have to pay, but in truth, they really resented not being treated in a superior position above fellow directors. Provide little duchies for idiots, spoil them with special benefits and expense accounts, and try to tell them they are equal to all other directors. Such a concept moistened their shorts!

My recommendation to those of you who wish to push forward to create something as wonderful as a national theatre, or any other valuable plan to America's well being, is to prepare for the corruption I guarantee will occur and/or tell the taxpayers, "This request is for four billion dollars, but if we add ineptitude and corruption you need to supply seven billion dollars. Do you still want this? And if you do, here are the parameters to protect you. Here are the ways that you will have the power to opt out of any program once it is discovered that the program has become corrupted. And here are the methods by which those who caused the corruption will be punished." Now is the time to rebuild the pillory in every town square.

The more troubles I confronted the greater became my perception. I saw things from different angles, even the enemy's points of view, and though I then knew clearly why they were wrong, and why their wrong could create no right, for anyone, I nevertheless checked my own dreams to test with greater objectivity my plans. I realized how odd from my childhood I not only wanted to save this world, as many children do, but I tried. If God couldn't do better what made me think I could. Grandiosity! Though, of course, if we each contribute a little here, a little there, it would all add up and perhaps . . . oh well, there I go again.

I also realized that at no time did it ever occur to me that I had to make the national theatre happen by myself. I only hoped to be a cog in the wheel. And that was blatantly stupid. Innocence has much stupidity coupled with it. If one of you choose to pick up these pieces know that you need to alter my methods. Under no circumstance assume that everyone wants what is good for our society. Once money is put on the table civility towards the common good is abandoned. I had too much idealism. Some is necessary. Too much is foolish. The hardest aspect as an idealist is the insults from your friends and enemies. They argue that you have gone mad; that you are wasting your time; that you are destroying your chances to succeed. They attempt to force you to live with injustice, which they insist is a necessary evil. But we must remind our selves how Hamlet persuaded Guildenstern and Rosencrantz to trust his sanity rather than to listen to the Queen and King.

Ham.   "My uncle-father and aunt-mother are deceived."

Guil.   In what, my dear lord?

Ham. I am but mad north-north-west.
When the wind is southerly, I know a hawk from a handsaw." (*Hamlet* II.2)

※

MAN HAS POWER to become a fully realized human being.

The journey of your Odyssey can succeed if you have no fear to live it. When you choose to fight for truth others will assume you are as mad as Hamlet. This can become confusing. To judge whether this madness is worth it ask your self what you want from life. I want theatre. I want family. I want America. I want collaborations with actors, designers, playwrights, audiences, critics, and dramatic literature. So I seek those things regardless of costs. I doubt there is any better way to experience life than to be inside my own story, struggling to create something of value. Starring within the play that is my life has been fantastic. I have no gripe. I simply realize what fools we are to take a great country and fuck it up. But I have no fear of Scylla and Charybdis because evils against me help to place me as the star within my own play and force me to find the solution, an existential journey. The further I participate into activism the closer I wind up in the center of my personal drama. It almost doesn't matter whether I fail or succeed. What matters is that by putting myself into the middle of my life I experience my existence, see more clearly the faults of our society, and if I am honest, discover truth about myself. My life then becomes a worthwhile play, my personal commitment within our art of men acting. That is how we rise above Scylla and Charybdis, so have no fear for fighting the evils that surround us. Fighting a good fight is the best choice one can make. I notice when I am in St. Peter's Basilica that statues of saints always look ready for war. They have muscles, weapons and a sense of genitalia while so many statues in American churches lack tits and ass, as if they have never lived on this earth. Take note.

※

I STAYED WITH ABC'S *Loving* and directed one awful script after another. Then word got around that I was a great television director, so

One Life to Live hired me. Can you imagine word spreading about my being a great soap opera director when frankly I didn't have the slightest clue what I was doing? I personally could only find pride in one out of seventy-five scenes. Otherwise I was embarrassed by the dishonesty of my work.

Two tech directors stopped me in the studio.

"We like the shows best when you direct."

I assumed they were goofing with me.

"What makes you say such a thing?"

"You bring reality to the show. We like that."

"You've seen reality on this show?"

"Well no, but you're the only one who tries."

And, of course, that was true, but only because I refused to skip reality to create the nonsense of the show's artificiality. I was trying to find some truth and I only find truth in life, not in escapism. Even when I directed the very first episode of *One Life to Live*, before the day was completed, Erika Slezak in that ABC studio was honoring me over the loudspeaker, "Tony Giordano is the best director this show has ever had." It is not my nature to brag about my talents, but it is my nature to be upset when anyone exaggerates my talents, and in television they always did. I had directed that show for character work and those actors were relating in ways rare on the show. So I accept praise for that aspect.

Then the producer told me there was only one slight flaw to the show, but she felt it was the lesser producer's fault, not mine, and certainly not hers.

"What was it?" I wanted to know.

"Kevin was sweating."

"Sweating?" I pursued, confounded by her statement.

"Yes, make-up should have wiped his face and never allowed the audience to see sweat."

"But," I insisted, "I caused him to sweat because I made his parents nail him for his bad behavior and I wanted the audience to know he was in pain."

"No, Tony, your work was great, but he should have had no sweat."

Need I elaborate further on the idiocy of soap opera?

I had made the error of signing a contract only because my lawyer said, "Tony, we know you well enough to know when you want out of that contract, you'll find a way." From then on, each exit sign became neon to me. After an excruciating season at *One Life*, apart from the joy of directing Erika Slezak and a few other actors, Linda Gottlieb, the producer, confronted me in the hallway.

"Tony, what do you think about our ratings? Aren't things getting so much better?"

I couldn't help myself.

"Linda, are you fucking crazy? Don't you watch the shit we're putting on television? Can you not understand what a crime we're committing to the minds of the American people?"

The blank look in front of her eyes revealed the blank look from the back of her brain. It was either that, or hitting her, so I guess I made the right decision. She terminated my contract.

❋

THE DAY AFTER MY FINAL SHOW with *One Life*, I received two phone calls from two separate theatres in Florida to direct two plays. Obviously, God hated *One Life* as well. The first was from Coconut Grove Playhouse to direct *I Hate Hamlet*. The second was from Palm Beach to direct *Gravity of Honey*, a new play.

I was back in theatre without the slightest knowledge of how this occurred. So, despite a seven-thousand-dollar difference in lesser salary, I took the challenging new play, *Gravity*, about a female performer whose body caves in and turns into a black hole as she frenetically writes complex physics formulas. I kept searching for the universality in the play but could find only the particular. Her problem seemed to lack a human element. So did my production.

❋

COCONUT GROVE OFFERED ME their next production, *Substance of Fire*, and as soon as I read it I jumped at it. What a great play. Robin Baitz has the pen to write plays that awaken truth. I found greatness in *Substance*. I cast it with Mark Margolis as the father, Mark Gaylord, Michael Mastrototaro (now known as Mastro), Nancy McDaniel, and Crista Moore. During auditions I had requested only big, strong, starring actors should audition for Isaac Geldhart. Somehow Mark Margolis got an audition, and he does not fit that description. He walked in surreptitiously, as if he was going to rob us, and I asked him if he was prepared to read the long monologue. He said yes, so I asked him to begin after I introduced him to the two producers, Arnold Mittleman and Lynne Peyser. Mark walked over to the window and read the monologue. I had to lean toward him to hear what he was saying. Apparently Lynne and Arnold never leaned forward. As soon as Mark finished, I thanked him and let him go. Then I turned to the producers and said, "Hire him, he's the Isaac Geldhart I want to work with." Both producers objected vehemently.

"You told us you wanted a big, strong man. He couldn't even be heard in this tiny room. We have an eleven hundred seat theatre."

"He's the one I want. He will be heard."

This led to several ridiculous moves until I made it as clear as possible that I would only do the show with Mark. This was odd considering I didn't know him, but I realized he understood that monologue as well as I did so I went to bat for him. To make a long story short, Mark and the four other great actors filled the theatre with comedy, romance, drama, and a great performance.

I was able to make the second act work, partly because I had a portrait painted of Isaac's dead wife and hung it upstage center facing the audience so she became Isaac's nemesis, reminding us that she wisely left her children 51 percent of the stock in her father's company. When I was back in New York I went to see *Substance* at Lincoln Center. The second act was flat, so I was able to realize why the reviews reflected its failure. But Baitz's play was not at fault. In act 2 it is urgent that the social worker find a tougher woman within herself and confront Isaac Geldhart so he is then able to rise above his lifelong limitation. Nancy was able to accomplish that. We won the *Carbonell Award* from the Florida critics.

✳

OFF TO NEW FRONTIERS! The blacklisting was encroaching. There was no way I could, or would stop it. And since I was never going to become a political person who gathers soldiers to fight his battles, knowing I live solely from the principles born out of thought and persuasion, I realized that as long as my truths, well executed, cannot awaken my opponents I told myself this world is an immense universe, time to move on. Fortunately I have courage. To me life is about joy. My childhood desire to sing and dance was to entertain a family in pain during WWII. It didn't matter that I could neither sing nor dance. My dream of a national theatre was to enlighten our society so we could develop a culture of joint experiences and respect for each other. It doesn't matter to me that I was inventing an idea and trying to execute it without tools to fulfill it, or the political savvy to raise money, gather soldiers and weapons and force it to happen. So, once all this failed, off I needed to go to find my new frontier since I believe in an eternity of God's love. What else was out there, beyond LORT Theatres, corrupt housing, the SSDC, the O'Neill, and all the lying from an industry that falsely called itself "Family"?

CHAPTER EIGHT

EVER SINCE I WAS A KID the word Ananke followed me. Out of nowhere it would pop up. When I researched the word I discovered that Ananke is the Goddess of necessity. She does all the hard work. In other words, God does not punish us, as most religions profess. Instead the soul simply has no other choice, at some point, but to improve itself either here or in the afterlife where the soul reigns eternal. There is no escape. We must pay. I first became fascinated with the word Ananke, when I discovered it in my high school Greek textbook. Then occasionally I would come upon it in strange places, as one day hitting tennis balls against a handball court I noticed A-N-A-N-K-E sprawled across two adjoining courts and I stopped to stare and ponder how this could be. It was my word, and no one else should have known about it, so I fancied that it was scrawled in chalk for me to take the time to meditate upon it. Through the years I researched its importance and learned that because Ananke is the goddess of necessity she forces us, without sentimentality, to resolve our wrongs, to kick our ass until we clean up our mess.

When I was a senior at Fairfield University I decided to visit the new library for the first time for no particular reason. I walked down its center lane, stopped at aisles on both sides of me, turned left, walked five feet, stopped, reached eye level and took a book, opened it instantly to a poem in French, by Pierre Jean Jouve, titled "Ananke."

Stunned, I stole the book.

I had to. You understand.

So yes, I confess to the guilt, I shoved the book in my shirt and rushed out of the library. After all, it really was mine. How could it not be?

ANANKE

Malheur à la méchaneceté de l'Europe!
Malheur aux nations d'orgueil dans la mer!
Malheur aux banlieues de pluie et aux mouvements d'acier,
Malheur à la race aggressive, à sa grossièreté par le monde!

Malheur à la population des ville aux cents gares!
Malheur aux têtes chenues dans les sorbonnes de clinquant!
Malheur à ce nid de pillards comme une excroissance de l'Ouest
Qui s'est proclameé à la plus haute branche des siècles!

Il sera dévoré, il sera confondu.
Sa plaine deviendra comme un os sans la chair,
Ses soldats et ses femmes seront asphyxiées dans leurs terriers,
Et la dorure tombera en rouille.

P. J. Jouve
(Anthologie Poetique du XX Siecle)

ANANKE

Curse the malice of mankind
Curse the nations strutting on the sea.
Curse the raining suburbs and tides of steel.
Curse war's blood, its gluttony against the globe.

Curse the city denizen to his subway stations.
Curse the white heads to their tinsel ivory towers.
Curse this nest of brigands, this dung heap the West.
Proclaiming itself the pinnacle of time.

It will be devoured. It will be abashed;
Its landscape a flayed bone,
Its generals pawing matrons choked in their hiding,
Its gilded face running to rust.

Guy Gallo
After P. V. Jouve

So I formed a corporation I call Ananke, Ltd, to write and produce products that enlighten our society. This is my new way around my old passion of national theatre.

My question is "How can we convince our society to correct itself and prevent its existence from slipping off its grid? Or, should we step aside and let our sun spin away, leaving Ananke in charge of the clean up?" These are the questions I ask myself ever since the flight back to New York after directing *Substance of Fire* at the now extinct Coconut Grove Playhouse. Once I fully realized that we'd lost America's innocence and I had fought as hard as I could to correct corruptions, but had lost, I had more and more reason to write.

CHAPTER NINE

FLYING BACK TO NEW YORK my childhood flashed before me with all of its nooks and crannies. Next morning I started to write a notebook of what I had recalled on the plane, but the first scene I wrote was a Coney Island beach scene and it was clearly filmic. By the end of the first week, I knew I was writing a screenplay. I felt overwhelming love for my characters. How odd, after so many years of theatre, that I should write a screenplay.

I wanted to dramatize how important it was to fight for my future because I want all children to recognize the importance of their future. And I wanted all grown ups to discover the world so they would know how important it is to take chances. The worse that can happen is you fail to achieve your goals but in reaching high you touch the stars while you inspect your personal odyssey. It all adds up.

Thus I entered the catastrophic journey into authorship.

Either our end days are near, as so many now predict, or at the very least we have dug our selves into a bind. Can America escape Scylla and Charybdis and rise out of its dilemma? I hope for a happy conclusion. Consistent with my respect for God, and my love of humanity I also hope the end of the world, as we know it, might mean we make this world better, caring about each other and putting our talents towards civilizing, as opposed to ending in destruction. Civilization has accomplished so much. Beginning in 1945, to celebrate being #1 for winning World War II, Americans created every conceivable luxury, personal advantages as infinite as the imagination, and the collective opportunity to forge our own world. We achieved material comforts with such exuberance that more than 50 percent of the adult population lost taste for education, thus manufacturing national illiteracy, while continuing to insist that we are #1. But in a country of three hundred and ten million people, no one rose as our poet, dramatist, composer, or philosopher.

We feel we do not need them since they question life. Besides, we already have the answers: money, sex, huge mansions, and splashy cars. We forfeit history by disdaining the past, convincing our selves that new is all that matters. To me progress is the intelligence to save the best of the past and combine it with the best of the present and future. This reminds me of a drive through Umbria, where the top of ancestral fortifications known as Centro are gathering places for the town folks, while new buildings embrace the surrounding cliffs. It is all so beautiful because it is filled with love, respect, and joy.

As my hair began to turn whiter, I realized that all my life I was tied by my umbilical cord to America, the country I love. No matter what problems are created by our society, we never seem to know how to blame all the causes at the same time. Until we can do that we will never fix the mess. The ability to see the full picture, objectively, is a good definition of why Bonn defined drama as the objective art of men acting.

Like Diogenes holding his lamp before him in search of that one honest man with the answers, I sought but could not find him or her. I learned in childhood to seek answers from very old Jews or very old Italians. They usually hit the target. So I asked Lydia Franklin, my old Jewish friend, how to find at least that one person. She told me, "Turn the lamp around to shine upon your own face. You may not find another." I took her advice and this coincided with my writing. I decided to search my life to locate my role within this historical context. I encourage everyone to join in, one big hootenanny of personal truth!

I entered this world relatively poor, though no one ever mentioned it when I was young. My family accepted life itself with gratitude and, of course, Italian food. The security I found in my background gave me the drive to fight for terrific experiences, so I know how important a good fight is. But many do not have a good enough background, so it is hard to make their life better. They don't even know the difference. To inspire others to have a good life, people need examples of how to reach into themselves for what is good, ergo, my passion for education and theatre. Helen Keller studied the Swedish philosopher, Emanuel Swendenborg. His work revealed to her that missing her senses should not prevent a full life because her soul has no limitations. Helen became a great human being. She told a friend, "Death is nothing more than going from one room into another, except when once I enter that room I will be able to see."

Unless we reach within ourselves to cure the ills of our society we would never be able to know and admit how we contributed to the dissolution of our American Dream. But, thanks to our Constitution, we have the incredible opportunity to forge any world we want, even now with our mess. Daily we invent ways to destroy our society, for greedy purposes, but this demonstrates to me how much power we have for what we want. Yet when it comes to fixing the ills of our society, we claim powerlessness. We journey to the moon or the bottom of the sea. But whenever issues of morality are brought up we claim man is never going to change, and worse, he can do nothing about this. So then we waste enormous sums of money on committees, organizations, foundations, charities and federal programs that are supposed to fix our problems. It is as fake as the pills people fool themselves into believing will make them healthy, rather than taking a walk, breathing God's air, and eating proper foods. We have power to cure or to destroy. It is our choice. And choice is the central most important element to create character in plays.

I dedicated major portions of my life to committees and, as I mentioned earlier, I discovered the majority of members on these committees are too frightened to perform with any value or often too corrupt. Because I never say die I have narrowed my goal from changing this world to simply sharing my truth in the hope of changing that part of the world I stand upon. Since we are reasonably unimportant people, at least as the notion of star power seems to go, we can write our own odyssey and benefit each other. Nowadays our movies are too clever. And rarely do our artists attempt even to interpret life, so busy are they performing in films of slick corporate takeovers, or 'send-up' cartoons. If enlightenment is to occur, it is now up to us to open our eyes, tell the truth, and not be afraid that we may make fools of ourselves.

I find the talent among the young to be very revealing. Young actors and actresses, as well as their counterparts in society are healthy, athletic, and gorgeous. They even have genuine talent. They grew up in basic comforts, travelled and vacationed beautifully when they weren't charging incredible sums of money for their education, sneakers, clothes and condoms. Now they are in charge. They earn huge salaries in Hollywood, on television, in government, Wall Street, designing, manufacturing, virtually anything they were trained to sell to our society. So, where's the beef? And why are they so angry? Why do they embrace hopelessness? For all their power show me any insights they have created that can fix our woes, other than lipstick, jewelry, diet pills, oxycodone. I already know what they believe because their universities have exposed their ideologies, but when I turn on my television and watch young, beautiful, talented people flying into space, and landing with weapons so they can conquer some country or corporation I simply wonder why they never seem to include any people in their characters. A beautiful actress in a long black gown, with a gun in her hand, does not make a worthwhile film that I want to see. And whenever they do try to reveal some humanity it more often than not is about someone who is demented. For all the expense it costs for these young people to grow up in America how come they have no life worth sharing and how come they seem so hateful. Cary Grant turned a difficult childhood into a fabulous, joyful career. And Ella Fitzgerald knew how to sing beyond her troubled teenage years. This is not only important because it is necessary, it is important because Cary and Ella rose to the height of their talent, which is the path all talent should take. Are we not tired of watching young people having sex on camera to turn on our aged society? Betty Davis made about sixty-four films, all of them about women we grew to know by the end of her films.

God forbid our education system should interpret life for students. Parents sue the schools for one foolish reason or another and force education to be about facts, figures, and preparation to enter the marketplace and maintain a failed society, instead of developing spiritual and aesthetic humanity in their sons or daughters. But these parents are people of the lie. They force their children to graduate from suffocating schools, enter the workplace as robots, and maintain the luxuries their parents are accustomed to.

From my point of view, the consistent fault that lies beneath our disasters has to do with our illiteracy. If we were a thinking society, and could analyze topics before we voted, shopped, or supported leaders, we would certainly be further along than we presently are. And for those who claim this is silly because man will never do all of this, I say, you don't deny the value of something just because not everyone will do it, and certainly not because those who chose to do this don't agree to do all of it. Improving ten percent more of our society would be of great value. We honor the one guy in the world who runs the fastest in the Olympics even though the rest of us rarely get off the couch.

Jeanne Dixon predicted I would rethink everything as we sat across from each other in the Mayflower Hotel having breakfast in 1981. She was right. Between the battles I waged nationally and time I was spending on my commitments to my family, I looked around and saw suffering rearing its ugly head everywhere, not only because of the people who were lying, as with my activist projects, but because of the plain old serious life problems that ordinary people face, as in my family. Life is hard. This might sound like a truly stupid thing for me to discover, and I guess it is. I've always known life is difficult. I am discovering just how hard it is to find solutions. It is time to remind ourselves that we need to help people become people. Instead of purchasing happiness by buying that perfect new car, beach house, or diamond bracelet it would be helpful to make this world have the values we need. Why not close all schools for five years and create a referendum towards a philosophy of education so that we can finally help students who, in turn, can help society. While writing *Brooklyn Odyssey* I amused myself daily that I was writing about a boy searching for education, rather than robbing banks or killing snakes. But at this moment I am grateful I fought for education. I remain adamant. Man can improve if, when and how he learns how to use the power of choice.

❊

AFTER MARRIAGE, four children, a nervous breakdown and the inevitable divorce, Theresa was diagnosed as schizophrenic. But unlike many families where their troubled relative roams the streets, my father and mother, along with my mother's sisters and brothers, found the solution. Theresa was protected due to their love, prayers and, as always, food. When Aunt Dottie, who lived on Staten Island asked Theresa, who lived in Bethlehem, Pennsylvania what she wanted and Theresa said corn beef on rye Aunt Dottie went to a New York deli, drove to Bethlehem and brought Theresa two huge corn beef sandwiches to let Theresa know someone cared. In time Theresa received shock treatments, which, coupled with the love of my aunts, parents, and Theresa's children, guided her to health and she returned to us. Theresa's youngest daughter, Lorraine, was on the battlefront during all the worst years. Lorraine was also the strongest of all of us. Somehow she could stand up to Theresa, who at her height of anger was powerful. During that awful time Theresa drove like a mad woman and had police chase her. I heard one story where she came to a screeching halt, jumped out of her car, chased by two policemen, hopped over a backyard wall, and wound up in a fistfight with the cops. Considering my childhood with Theresa, I wasn't surprised. However, the years of anger now created breast cancer. Sad as this story is, I tell it to point out two things. First, the family kept guard until she recovered. Two, their love and their food cured her.

Theresa recovered, and during her final years with cancer we became friends. After a lifetime of angst, Theresa wrote wonderful letters to everyone. Her higher nature survived and revealed who she really was underneath her sickness. How grateful I am to my family for sustaining my sister's life. And you might say how sad that she then died, but I felt her life followed the journey, in a narrow sense, of King Lear, who also had to go through the trials of a storm to locate the truth that prepared him for his death. I am committed to the belief that the worst possibility is to kick your sick one into the street, as so often happens in our society. Sick people are a terrible burden on their families, I agree. But thrown into society, they are a burden without love, prayer, or food. Family is the ultimate art of men acting when it's real family, at which point it becomes sanctified.

We need to help lift life whenever possible.

Even when I was directing a simple, lightweight romantic comedy called *Mixed Emotions* at Broadway's Golden Theatre, I tried to infuse as much value into the romantic notion of a loving older couple, thankfully played by Katherine Helmond and Harold Gould, real pros. The play was weak but at least positive. I was tired of the theatre of cruelty, which makes you feel, after the first act, that life isn't worth living. There is no excuse for theatre to be so negative. Unlike film or television where there is little process since time is of the essence and cameras and studio costs are rising with each tick of the clock, in theatre you have time to get to know the material, think things through and alter your approach through the three or four weeks of rehearsal. In addition, during previews when you watch the audience, you can rehearse the next day and make moments more significant. In theatre you can even change the entire approach to the show, with good notes, hours before the opening. Once you build the foundation in the production and have explored the action with the actors and their characters, the entire show can be adjusted. And if you know how to give that one significant note for a new approach, you can sit back and watch your show take on new laughs, and newer emotions than you had the previous performances.

During the two weeks of previews of *Snow Orchid* in New York Olympia Dukakis told me she never saw a director take more chances than I do during previews. And I guess I do, but it is easy to be creatively flexible when you have such talents to work with as Olympia and Peter Boyle. Once the show opens, it remains steady because the exploration is finished. In contrast, a soap opera shoot is horrifying. By the time I could feel the right way to approach several scenes, they were taped and there was no way to recover the mess. The art of life is more like theatre than soap opera, because if you use all the tools at our disposal, never give up, you can alter trouble. You have to care. And you have to try many things to come to the right conclusion. Life and theatre require the willingness to admit faults so you can find the truth that will create success.

CHAPTER TEN

UTA HAGEN CALLED. She asked me to direct her and Fritz Weaver in three one-act plays written by Vincent Canby. One of them I had already directed years earlier for *Earplay* radio called *After All,* and it had never been aired because after the taping with Nina Foch and Keene Curtis, it turns out the producer had never acquired the rights. Fifteen years later, Uta called and asked me to direct that same play about a married couple undressing for bed at the end of the day of their seventy-fifth wedding anniversary, a charming and wonderfully funny piece.

Of course I said yes. What strange synchronicity for this play to be waiting for me all these years and now with other such primary players. Fritz is a wonder who has dedicated great time, energy, and talent to our profession. Uta is a legend, perhaps less talented than her celebrity, but nevertheless an actress to be reckoned with. And Vincent was a sweetheart. His second play took place in hell and was very surrealistic, needing enormous readjustment, which I provided to the delight of Uta, who kept telling the others I was a genius. The third play took place on a South American island during a revolution. I had been telling Uta that her choices for this island play were too internal. She needed to be less lyrical and more overt, which was odd because her limitations were almost always the opposite.

The day we began to perform the island play came first and no one responded in the audience to the humor because Uta was completely internal. So I went back to speak with her and Fritz.

Uta was disturbed.

"Why did no one laugh?"

"They couldn't hear you."

"Couldn't hear me. That is not possible."

"They couldn't hear you."

"I have never acted in my life where people could not hear me."

"You just did."

"How can you keep insisting they couldn't hear me?"

"Uta, I was among them, for Christ's sake, and I couldn't hear you. And I know the play. What the hell do you think I'm doing here if you can't even accept the basic reality I know when someone can hear an actor or not."

Well, you would think I had smacked her in the face, judging from her horrified look. I was no longer a genius. Funny how whimsically appellations among theatre folk come and go. That night she performed that act wonderfully well. So I went immediately to their dressing room and told them how tremendous they were. Uta, stubbornly refused to give in.

"I just spoke louder."

"No, you opened up your character's thoughts and communicated them to Fritz. The audience was then able to hear why they should respond. Then they laughed."

I hated to give the preeminent acting teacher an acting lesson, but there it was nevertheless. Legends often get to their esteem by preventing anyone from intruding on their legend. I'm too basic for such silliness. I like to hear actors.

Fritz, suspecting trouble, chimed in.

"Thank you, Tony, for your notes this afternoon. They were wonderful and really helped tonight's performance."

Later, Fritz took me aside.

"Clearly, Tony, you have no sense of diplomacy."

I'll buy that.

※

I WAS INVITED TO OBSERVE *Law and Order*, which was shooting in a studio on the river on West 22nd Street. So I went and watched, bored out of my mind. Too dry a process for my taste, and from what I was watching, there was rarely anything to direct since most of the action and the needs of the characters were fairly pro forma. But Mary Joan Negro Snow is my great friend who lives in California. If it were not for each other, we'd both be in the booby hatch by now. Mary Joan starred in one of the episodes of *Law and Order* just before my observing. She told the producer, Joe Stern, who owned the Matrix theatre in LA that I was the director who could invent a way to do double casting, which, LA actors had dreamed about but didn't know how to create.

LA actors love money and therefore LA. They also love theatre, but they can't afford the time to be in a play every night when they might be able to do a day's shoot, or several days, or more. Could I find the way to fix this problem? My answer naturally was "Of course," always searching for a new theatrical thrill. Stern told me he was leaving *Law and Order* and returning to run his Matrix theatre. Would I invent a way to fulfill double casting at his theatre? He said he had a small core of an acting company.

As soon as I hear an interesting idea I always forget to check it with skepticism. A psychic, Tula, once told me, you were born with total openness to the entire universe. My mother seemed to realize this about me. "All I ever hear on this end of the phone from you is 'Yes I'll be there.' You never say no to anything."

I spoke to Joe twice weekly. During this phase of my career I had clearly begun to realize how the not for profit theatre was unwilling to create a national theatre, so I began to crave an acting company. I told Joe I would only be interested in this project if we could put together an ongoing company. I would work with the company that we would begin to form with this production. I believed that once it was easy for talented actors to do theatre but remain available to film and television LA would have an interesting acting company.

I would develop the company for six months each year and continue to freelance the remainder of the time. I would pick a play that was difficult, otherwise the challenge would not be proven. I would then direct the double cast as if there was only one production. No actor would be the understudy to any other actor. I would block the show in such a way that whenever an actor got a job for a day or more he or she simply had to contact the other actor who played the same role and ask whether the other actor was free to take over the necessary number of shows, then contact the stage manager and finalize the plan. No one else needed to be contacted, and all the other actors in the show would be comfortable because every actor was directed to be in the same show.

Most of our long-distance calls were challenging because Joe Stern couldn't imagine my idea working. Why did I feel so confident it could work, he would ask. And over and over again, I would go through the idea, even making him understand that I would block the entrances and exits exactly the same for each of the two characters playing that one role, but permit some movements slightly differently depending upon the needs of each actor within the meat of the scene. I even planned on different costumes for each actor, so no actor carbon copied the other. In other words, I was, as per my wont, playing Theatre. Joe said he could not conceive that such a thing could ever work.

Then, despite a killer flu that should have put me in a hospital, I flew to LA to speak to Richard Baer for rewrites prior to rehearsals of *Mixed Emotions* on Broadway and to meet with the core group of Matrix actors who wanted to be part of the double casting experiment but had doubts about the process I was establishing. I was scheduled to stay at Richard Baer's condo, and after I arrived I went into his guest bedroom for twenty hours and slept off the flu.

When I finally came out of my stupor, I discovered Richard was not a re-writer, and since he had a much too weak, shallow romantic comedy, it needed major work. He seemed stunned and unable to do much about this. Then I went to a meeting with the core of Matrix actors to explain the way my method for double casting would work. They agreed with Joe that my idea seemed impossible but found I had conviction. They had assumed double casting meant two casts, two separate productions, like the A and the B Companies, or one cast with understudies. I made it clear this would always be only one production. Reluctantly they agreed. I told them to read *The Tavern* because I felt it would be a true challenge. The large cast, doubled, came to thirty actors, and the play was a period piece known to be a melodramatic farce, so we needed to learn style and form, and maintain one well put together production. It was a thrilling challenge, the kind of theatre I crave.

※

I FLEW BACK TO NEW YORK to complete pre-production sets, lights and costumes of *Mixed Emotions,* nervous that no rewrites were yet coming, and found out simultaneously that Joe and the core of actors at the Matrix did not like *The Tavern*. They felt it was not important enough. But *The Tavern* is theatre, par excellence, written by a man who was an actor/manager, George M. Cohan, who tried desperately to prevent Actors Equity from being formed in 1920. I was connected to his feelings seventy years later, for I too was fighting the concept of such a labor union. I had become aware that artists allow their creativity to be stymied by their need to be parented by unions, when actors and actresses should be the high priest and priestesses of theatre, not children needing tit.

My ideals make miracles happen and everyone enjoys miracles, like, for instance, the creation of subsidized housing at Manhattan Plaza. So, with my conviction about ideals being convincing I flew back to LA to explain to the core of actors why I had mapped it out in such an ideal process. What I did not tell them, because I felt I would have to prove this by directing the play, was that the play sings to me in a unique way. It has a sense of universality because it stretches its humor across classes and treats the central action virtually as a metaphor for the world itself. At this point of my career such a notion meant a great deal to me, the very opportunity to direct a sense of the world as I see it. All the new plays I was directing were making me itch for unique experiences. And double casting thirty actors into one melodrama/farce/drama was the great challenge I craved.

※

SIMILARLY, the O'Neill Playwrights Conference was the ideal environment for me. Because of the spirit of a hot summer writing festival there was opportunity to experiment with ways to present scripts with a certain improvisational manner. The work at the conference was pure as possible, even though Artistic Directors and producers came to shop plays. And tourists came from everywhere. The O'Neill was a spotlighted environment! But Lloyd knew the importance of playing sides against the middle, and because I did not, I was his perfect director. I never bothered with politics at the conference for which I hardly take credit, since I never politic. In my opinion Lloyd did his best to maintain a hands off from commercialism, until he ensnared himself inside his paradoxical contradiction, a Scylla and Charybdis of his own making, once he met August Wilson and climbed down from the fence he balanced himself upon to reveal his commercial lust.

I met Lloyd in 1975, with the world premiere of *Put Them All Together* when I welcomed dawn in Chapel Hill waiting for a gas station to open while my playwright was smashing all the glass in her accommodations, causing my leading lady to walk the streets barefoot to save her life. So much great drama happens offstage. I cancelled rehearsals for the day. Lloyd Richards flew in from New York to see the opening, and one hour after the curtain came down he hired me to direct at the O'Neill National Playwrights Conference, a job that continued for eleven years.

Lloyd gave repetitive speeches. One in particular was our obligation to use the O'Neill only for creativity, not business, so the environment would be conducive to good work. It was the right concept, in the spirit of genuine not-for-profit. This was the reason I spent so much time with Lloyd for we shared the purity of this belief and our joint interest in interracial casting across the color divide. As I stated, I found in Lloyd a man who seemed committed to theatre rather than show business. I assumed that together we could gather the forces necessary towards a national theatre. Unfortunately, the very first thing I was told about Lloyd was *"Beware, Lloyd speaks with forked tongue"*. In time I saw this for myself. But I also saw his value. Lloyd and I became best friends, or at least we tried. We respected each other, but we were often irritated by each other, similar to my relationship with my sister, Theresa.

But for as long as Lloyd was true to his mandate to keep the conference separate from commercialism, I was convinced the conference was my road to the sun. It should have been. It could have been. It almost was. But it broke its mission once Lloyd abandoned his conscience by taking August Wilson through the secret garden to success, from the O'Neill to Yale to Broadway, with the ease of parading a child through an unguarded candy store. What made this unacceptable were all the years Lloyd professed that the O'Neill needed grants because it existed not to sell tickets but to prepare plays to be distributed across America to not-for-profit theatres. Lloyd abandoned every ounce of his own objections when he took August Wilson away from Helen Merrill, Wilson's agent. I left at that point, knowing the O'Neill was infected. I never revealed my reason for quitting, but one day in New York City

Helen Merrill stopped me. "We all know why you left the O'Neill, Tony. What Lloyd swore, you practiced. What a shame he couldn't do the same." This observation of Lloyd awakened in me my insight of how easy it is for good people to betray their own standards once the chance arrives. Power and money are hard to turn down, but if you want to live by ideals, turning down such power and money is essential.

Much has been written about the conference's greatness for developing plays, but I believe history will not agree. Its greatness, frankly, was taking our community of actors, directors, and writers out of the city and letting us confront extraordinary script challenges in rapid improvisational rehearsals, sit and argue on the porch at dinnertime (usually with disgruntled actors wondering which idiots chose these terrible scripts as I would raise my hand to confess), then take a swim in the Connecticut Sound. So, I repeat for emphasis, that good people who contribute to evil are not always intrinsically evil. They mostly do the right things. But they contribute to the mess rather than clean it up. They assume that by hiding from everyone, particularly themselves, while they permit wrongdoing, they will never have to pay a price.

CHAPTER ELEVEN

EENY, MEENY, MINY, MO

RATHER THAN ENUMERATE all the individuals I met along the way, those who betray society's taxes, and misuse jobs they are hired to perform, I classify them as Eeny, Meeny, Miny, Mo. For the idealists among you, who might begin your work now, be aware that many people you meet along the way are faceless clichés of each other, papier-mâché figures who are hard to detect but who create our wicked world. That is why I stack them up behind each other. They lack individuality. The most egregious among them I will mention by name because their faces have yet to evaporate from my mind.

What is most painful is that the majority of these faceless people are friends, people I like. Good people, I repeat, who contribute to evil are not totally evil. They mostly do the right things. They want to fix the world. They love it when someone else does anything good for them. But they fail to help our world because they are always aware of the cost, and paying a price to cure ills has never been in their plan. They make the mess rather than clean it up and assume that by hiding while they perform 'only tiny' inroads into evil they will never pay a price. Welcome home, Ananke! Some of these faceless people take leadership positions without sufficient talent to do the job. So when they're up against the wall, they cheat, one way or another, to cover for their inadequacies. So by using Eeny, Meeny, Miny, Mo I will attempt to define their similarities, and demonstrate how they prevent not for profit theatre from attaining prophetic enlightenment.

❋

EENIES are the leaders who grab the gold ring. In my experience Eenies become artistic directors of not-for-profit theatres and managers of subsidized housing. They exist wherever taxpayers are foolish enough to supply money. The Eenies are usually educated beyond their moral capacity, born out of Marxist philosophy with capitalist bank accounts.

Eenies find no contradiction in receiving taxpayer money to run not-for-profit theatres while their eyes are glued to commercial profits, so they simultaneously work in their theatrical duchies for both the kind of salaries CEO's earn in business, hire themselves in their not-for-profit theatres to direct plays with future commercial contracts, and argue at the same time that they shouldn't pay union assessments. Once the show crosses into commercialism, Eenies benefit personally by earning commercial salaries, which they do not share either with their theatres or the taxpayers. Somehow in America, taxpayers are treated as Johns who hire whores but never receive any of the benefits and are always bypassed when pimps take their cut and the John is left with blue balls. No one treats taxpayers as shareholders, despite their enormous contributions for not-for-profit services.

Eenies see no contradiction in seeking under-the-table enhancement money from producers who surreptitiously initiate commercial productions in the not-for-profit theatres. Enhanced monies are used for special sets, like a lake at Lincoln Center that might cost two hundred thousand dollars. What is worse is that these producers then claim the show they are moving to Broadway doesn't require Broadway contracts because it is a regional production on tour to Broadway. The cost of the lake is then itemized as a gift from some one donor and kept out of the capitalization so actor salaries remain on a regional scale to avoid Broadway salaries.

When valuable producers like Liz McCann or Fred Zollo railed against such not-for-profit practices, they were condemned as having no interest in developing theatre. In fact, McCann and Zollo are the very producers who have the talents and taste to make true theatre. In comparison, too often the corrupt methods used by the not-for-profit Eenies provided inadequate revivals of plays originally produced on Broadway with superior professionalism by Liz McCann and her fellow commercial producers. Once every fifteen years the *New York Times* makes believe they care about all this by writing inept articles with no teeth.

"Wake up!" Robert Frost shouts from his grave. "I told you so. Why won't anyone listen?"

Eenies in Manhattan Plaza's HUD housing, as I mention previously, corrupted the section 8 subsidy artists acquired from the taxpayers. These Eenies instantly turned a sour gaze on the performing artists, regretting they had entered into this relationship, and forever after treated residents with disrespect. My letters to Senators Clinton and Schumer to investigate these corruptions, particularly of the missing 169 section 8 contracts, was as valuable as shouting up my own asshole.

In contrast, Ellis Rabb's APA (Association of Producing Artists) is an honorable example of a quasi-national theater. His is the name of a talented individual. Rabb's company toured across the United States. It was the first American repertory company on Broadway since Eva Le Gallienne's Civic Repertory Theater in the 1930s. Ellis and his company "Made popular comedies seem like classics and made difficult classics accessible to a general public." Ellis said, "I firmly believe that the only true strength and purpose of theater is its function as a mass-audience medium." He proved (in his words) "That Pirandello can be as widely appealing as George S. Kaufman" (Bio of Rabb).

There you have it. One man, with one great acting company, provided our best theatre and almost created a national theatre in the process. Ellis Rabb was not an Eeny because he had a face, individuality, a reputation, talent, and true professional biography. Of course, he needed not-for-profit support for his company but he provided valid justification for such support, i.e., prophetic good work. His stars are legendary: Rosemary Harris, George Grizzard, Ellis Rabb, Nancy Marchand, Jason Robards, Colleen Dewhurst, and just about everyone else who ever walked the stage for him. He produced a vast theatre of great plays: *The Importance of Being Earnest, Hamlet, A Life in the Theatre, The Royal Family, You Can't Take It with You, The School for Scandal, The Tavern, Man and Superman, Right You Are, The Show-Off,* Ghelderode's *Pantagleize, Exit the King, War and Peace,* Gorky's *Enemies.*

Ellis Rabb created the acting company that should have become the model for more companies. But, rumor abounds, that because of Robert Brustein, Ellis Rabb's company was denied grants for 'Lacking a political agenda' and thus put out of business.

Brustein, the academic Earle of Eeny, drew taxes from two not-for-profit movements, the National Endowment for the Humanities (since he was a professor at Yale, then Harvard) and the National Endowment of the Arts (since he was artistic director at Yale, then Harvard). With so much power and an academic disdain for commercial theatre, Brustein had a direct link to the endowments so he could recommend grants to support his favorite companies. But Brustein decided that the APA was not worthy, because he felt the APA had no political agenda. So once we lost the APA company Brustein produced plays with political concepts. He might even be credited with instigating the movement to deconstruct plays, thus altering them, rather than dramatize our humanity.

I concur with Robert Frost that art must pass through the marketplace to become art. Because once you fund art, or education, through a bureaucracy you vitiate the product due to the standards created by that bureaucracy in order to receive financing. The only standard should be excellence in art, theatre, and education. I spent eleven years on the final selection committee of the Eugene O'Neill Playwrights Conference to choose sixteen plays for each summer. It was quickly apparent that others on the committee were making decisions based on future grant proposals, to prove the O'Neill was democratic. "Tony, you are correct. This script fails to have substance, but that is precisely why it needs the O'Neill. Besides, the author is a blind lesbian who works in a diner in Alabama. We've never had one of those before." I confess exaggeration, but not by much.

Paradox rears its ugly head. In the late '90s, Brustein cried because his ART Company at Harvard was denied funds for, if my memory serves me, failure to create 'socially relevant' theatre. And Brustein argued this injustice, as he had once years earlier argued that a terrible review of his wife was the cause of her suicide, which might have been, but how often had he attacked so many actors without the conscience or concern he then, properly, showed his wife? Too many Eenies who grab the gold ring develop copper poisoning, apparently.

Once the NEA had been created to bring not for profit theatre across America it established peer panels to determine those worthy enough to receive the funds. But these peer panels were comprised of leaderships from the not for profit theatres who alternated every two years with parallel peer panels from other theatres. Since one hand feeds the other and since people who are not original thinkers follow the leader by playing 'simple Simon says', attempts were made to inject political agendas or social relevance into plays, which infected the productions and often eliminated universality from the heart and soul of the human condition, but sounded good on the grant proposal, accommodating a sense of democracy. Due to such democratic stories, plays began to represent town hall meetings where one disenfranchised socially relevant group after another took the stage to bitch about their awful suffering in this uncaring society. Women, blacks, Jews, gays, et al dramatized a need for reparation for their lives. Robert Frost turns over in his grave because we refused to listen to his warnings. To find theatre that honored the universal human condition producers flew to England to shop. Eeny artistic directors put their efforts into the thing they claim to hate most, attempts to use tax free not for profit money to find a play to direct on Broadway.

※

LLOYD RICHARD, I am sad to say, I would have to dub King Eeny. He was one of the founders of the Society of Stage Directors and Choreographers. His testimony helped create the illegitimate SSDC labor union for directors because he testified under oath that directors could not be independent contractors since "Producers sit at our side on a daily basis and dictate the director's choices." This is odd, I repeat, since I directed over forty productions for Lloyd and only once, because I insisted, did he ever even enter my rehearsals. Lloyd was a founder of SSDC's national labor union and an ex-president who fought to maintain its "One for all, all for one" brotherhood until he became artistic director at Yale and subsequently fought against the union in conjunction with other artistic directors who demanded exemption from assessments, this time arguing, through that forked tongue of his, that when artistic directors direct they are not labor, but management. I wonder how often you can argue both sides of every topic before you should tell yourself "I am full of shit."

I knew Lloyd better than anyone else in the theatre, and Lloyd knew me better than anyone else. We respected each other and grated against each other. We could have accomplished a great deal together if we could have erased the irritation we brought out in each other. It had to do with submission. Lloyd needed to be Buddha, and I only admire the aristocracy of quality and talent. For me we are otherwise always equal. The obligation to bow down and obey exists in some country I would never inhabit. Lloyd sat in state in his Buddha pose whenever he met with anyone, as armor, because he was basically insecure. When he became Dean of Yale's school of drama, people would ask me to help them learn how to deal with him, saying, "You're his best friend. Tell us how to deal with him." And I believe I was his best friend. I certainly saw value in him, but even George Washington knew how to let go of the mantle and refuse the title of King. After all, he apparently said, "What else did we fight for?" So I hated Lloyd's need for position. Lloyd hated my insubordination. Otherwise, we were best friends.

※

I RETURNED TO LA for a second pre-production trip. To force rewrites for Mixed Emotions I told the playwright we would work every morning from six a.m. All we achieved was a theatrical element to at least make the audience look at something. So while this elderly couple joke with each other through their romance, two movers take all the furniture out of her expensive New York apartment until both characters are left in its attractive emptiness to make their final decision. The play remained lightweight. Secondly, I held a reading of *The Tavern* at the Matrix, followed by a meeting with the core company, and won them over.

※

THEN, I returned to New York to direct *Mixed Emotions*, which, with gratitude to Katherine Helmond and Harold Gould, was a very pleasant experience, similar to enjoying an operation thanks to the drug. It may seem odd to enjoy a job knowing its limitations. But, one must make a living.

※

SO, HOPING TO CREATE A COMPANY similar to Ellis Rabb's, which was my only purpose for going to LA, I left New York the day after *Mixed Emotions* opened for what would be a very long rehearsal period. We needed this production to prove our worth, depending upon the success of the show. This would then help us fund an expansion for the double casting idea in a larger LA venue to develop a company.

Upon my arrival, I got my first wake up-call that there was trouble. There were three LA newspaper articles about the production. In each article Joe discussed his concept (which, of course, was mine) for double casting and how it would work (mine again). In one of the articles, I was referred to peripherally as the director he hired to do this. I confronted Joe. It was urgent LA know our plan and judge us accordingly so that when they reviewed the show they would also judge its possible continuance as an ongoing company. But our next conversation was appalling.

Joe said the papers simply left out all the things he told them. But that was odd because they captured, clearly, all the things I had told Joe. In talking this over, I realized Joe was a non-believer. He didn't want to go out on a limb because he suspected this experiment would fail, so he was securing publicity for having invented the concept. I then realized that I had to prove that my plan would work, without Joe's confidence. What irony! I had conceived the idea. I had convinced Joe and the core of actors. I had arrived at personal energy and expense. Now I had to dig into myself not just to make the show successful, but to prove the idea was worthwhile. I considered the red eye back to New York but I had already brought the designers into the project, and was in contact with actors. So I decided I had to stay and do the job. I had only one reason to leave, and that was due to the fact that Mary Joan Negro Snow pulled out. She needed more money and couldn't dedicate herself to this work. I was devastated, because she was the engine that began the idea between Joe Stern and me.

I cast actors from among LA's finest, thanks to Joe who had their phone numbers. These were the second bananas of TV and films, the ones with New York theatre backgrounds who longed for this double casting to work so they could benefit from it in the future. So, despite Joe's fears, and Mary Joan's absence, I knew my ideas were worth pursuing. I have always maintained an ability to know in advance how well something will work. I have a good sense of reading a play, thanks to Fr. Bonn. And once I mapped out the plan to rehearse a double cast, I was thrilled with the challenge.

Joe is the perfect example of an Eeny. He is a nice guy. That is why he and others are undetectable until it's too late. You trust them with your heart and soul, not to mention your best ideas. When they betray your agreed upon plans, you see them for what they are. Then it becomes impossible to maintain a friendship. They've revealed their bottom line.

God must have infused me with special DNA for my love of actors because I joy in helping them discover, develop, and perform. The rehearsals of *The Tavern* were nothing short of Christmas every day. These talented actors were so thirsty, they drank in every drop of truth provided to them, and they not only blossomed in their own development but watched the development of their fellow actors. Then they enjoyed the process of how I was creating individual characterizations for each actor yet retaining respect for the play's characters. Yes to theatre, wonder of wonders!

And, one by one, these actors would side up to me to say, "I had no idea this play was so great, but what you're bringing out of it is sensational." Yes, love, love, love makes the world go round, and a good rehearsal is the ability to create a world filled with love. In fact the director has the opportunity to set the tone for whatever reality he wants. It is easy to fantasize how to do the same for the world.

I've enjoyed eighty percent of my productions throughout the years. Ten percent were a mixed bag. And the remaining ten percent were horrifying. Not bad on the whole! During rehearsals for *The Tavern* when I would say, "Where's Lindsay? I'm ready for her scene," she would inevitably be in the kitchen, cleaning the oven, the refrigerator, everything. It was fascinating how the actors found a home for themselves hanging out for those nine weeks. They were always within reach and Lindsay Crouse, for whatever reason, took the position of housekeeper. Cotter Smith was delicious in his taste for this work. Julia McKenzie was sexy because she was so feminine and taught me a major costume trick. I hired Alan Armstrong to design the costumes because my costumier from *Curse of the Starving Class* at Yale was able to create clothes appropriate to each character. Her name was Dunya Ramicova, and I loved working with her. She was not available for *The Tavern,* so she suggested Alan.

First I met with Alan and discussed my idea of the show, going through each of the characters and talking about how they function in the production. I made it clear that in most cases I was searching for clothes, not costumes. Then I met with Alan and each actor separately. Well, Julia was playing the repressed daughter of the governor, who arrives unexpectedly at this haunted tavern to get out of a storm and has a naughty, though innocent, eye on the Vagabond. Julia explained that because she would be in long dresses, and in the second act a nightgown, it would be very valuable for her to feel sexy if we would provide a full corset underneath. Julia claimed as an actress it would give her that added sense of self because, as Julia explained, a corset presents everything nice a girl should enjoy about herself. She was transcendental in the performance, as was Anna Gunn, another beauty, who played the same role in a separate corset. Both actresses took me back in time to the best ingénue performance I ever saw, Rosemary Harris' Alice in Ellis Rabb's *You Can't Take it with You.*

To direct *The Tavern* requires a good deal of trust, because the dialogue in the first act is sparse, and if you rush through it you cannot set up the fun of the second act. These actors trusted me. I would drive to Sherman Oaks at night, watching Malibu fires shooting fifty feet into the air and spraying ash on top of my car. And relish life.

Neil Jampolis created a tremendous tavern and Jane Reisman lit the show to perfection. I called Trinity Rep and had them send the sound tape of fabulous thunderclaps, which is a major aspect of the show. Unfortunately, Joe Stern had a married couple as his production staff. The husband was the tech director, the wife the stage manager. Well, tech for *The Tavern* is elaborate, due to the storm, which must be a major character and continuous. There is also rain and lightning accompanying the thunder. So, I worked on tech for three nights. When finished I attempted a run-through of all the cues. I found myself yelling up to the booth, "No, that's not it, it should be the harsher clap!" Finally I stopped the tech to question the entire process. Then a crewmember in the booth explained that the tech director had never recorded any of the sound levels during the three nights of tech.

I have often suspected I will murder someone one day and this moment at the Matrix came close. I did threaten to kill him while Joe Stern stood by, fearing I would. The tech director's wife, my stage manager, was a dingbat. In all my years of directing shows, she was by far the worst stage manager in the history of stage-managing. She wrote none of the required indications in her book, so she had no way to call any of the cues, even if her husband would have recorded sound levels. They were perfectly matched as a couple. How lucky for them! But I had a show on its way to success, and I had two people bent on destroying it. Stupidity plays a role in theatre's art of men acting, since theatre at its core is human. Fortunately the crew person in the booth also knew a sound guy who could rush over and work with me throughout the night, redoing each of the cues, as I helped the dingbat write out her stage manager's production book and explain how to call the show. By afternoon we were able to tech with the actors and preview successfully that night. "Beware the jaws that bite, the claws that catch!" (Lewis Carroll).

The thirty actors were a dream brought to life. Every hour of every day was filled with creative discovery. Actors would even watch the other actor who was playing the same role and realize that I was not directing anyone to imitate anyone else. Everything was organic and their response to the play was thrilling, for they came to see that they could enter a tavern from a storm and become a universe that represented our world. Every one of these talented actors flourished in this work.

The show opened and was reviewed to great acclaim. The morning of the *LA Times* review, Joe Stern called and suggested he and I should talk about our future. Now he thought it would be a good idea to create the company I had hoped for. But I wasn't going to continue with him. I'd stayed to do the job as a professional for nine weeks, and I am grateful that it turned out so well, for I loved the cast and certainly I love the show. But I cannot allow myself to make believe we could work any further. The humanity of the work is what I live for. Several of Joe Stern's oldest friends were upset with me that I had this attitude, and they seemed to have no interest in knowing how I had come upon it. I believe a good man like Joe Stern could have become my partner, but the projects I crave require a partner who is always your partner. So I had to leave. Joe's supporters wanted me to stay, benefit from my success, and make nice/nice. When I asked what I would get from this success, they answered, "Television." I yelled, "Taxi!" Then sped to the airport.

In my absence, the show played six months through fires, earthquakes, and mudslides. Friends told me it lost its luster with every replacement Joe pushed into the show and, of course, the dingbat stage manager had no ability to maintain quality. And I hate myself for having to admit my weakness for people, but I truly liked the gal who was the stage manager. To make matters worse I truly liked Joe Stern, the perfect example of one of those people who are worth liking but you must always remember not to dream with them, hard to do when you live as a gypsy as I do depending upon the kindness of strangers. Within my final days in L.A. the dingbat suggested we play some tennis since I had no time to play during the long rehearsal. Five minutes into watching her be unable to hit the first ball over the net helped me to appreciate the goodness of her heart, which gave me a healthy laugh to get off the court, grateful for her sweet attempt.

CHAPTER TWELVE

MEENIES sign the checks, which gives them a false sense that they create the money. These are often the managing directors in not-for-profit theatres.

Some of these Meenies plot to take over an Eeny job.

The following is a two-for-one I witnessed during three-years in the '80s when I directed nine shows for Adrian Hall at both Trinity Rep in Providence, Rhode Island, and Dallas Theatre Center in Texas. Though he is an artistic director Adrian Hall is not an Eeny, for Adrian has talent to run a theatre, direct plays, gather an acting company of wonderfully talented actors, designers and stage crew. Adrian is real theatre because he is real.

I was usually in one of his two theatres while Adrian was at the other. In each theatre, Adrian had a managing director, i.e. two Meenies. During the times I was near these two I found them to be opportunists, but I never spoke to Adrian about this, mainly because Adrian seemed satisfied. In fact, so satisfied that he had each of these Meenies represent him at board meetings, which Adrian detested.

In time, Adrian was fired from each of his theatres.

Yes, you are ahead of me. These Meenies became the artistic directors of his two theatres.

But know that a Meeny cannot outplay an Adrian Hall. These two young men were now Eenies, but they had none of what it takes to do a job belonging to a true artistic director.

No, this time you aren't ahead of me.

Within approximately eight months of their new positions, each of them died.

Truly!

Died!

And each of them was only in his thirties, hardly old age! I am not assuming Adrian had anything to do with their demise, only that I feel you should never step into a position you are incapable of fulfilling. Methinks the soul can smell its own shit and doesn't like it.

CHAPTER THIRTEEN

MANHATTAN PLAZA CREATED A PARALLEL MESS. Our ad hoc committee spent two years creating paperwork, composing rules and regulations to provide equal opportunity to everyone in our constituency. These proposals for the subsidy were close to perfection. They included the purest and most honest reason for taxpayers to provide financing, and hopefully the residents would then add luster to Hell's Kitchen, which had for a long time been in degradation.

Once we completed the paperwork Rodney Kirk was hired to become the manager. He was a Meeny. And Irv Fisher, the owner, a Meeny. Laila Long of Housing, Preservation and Development also a Meeny. As soon as the subsidy was legally established, these Meenies stole 169 apartments off the subsidy, to rent to friends and associates. They violated the Board of Estimate's Determination that had established 100% section 8 contracts for the entire complex to be used only within three defined categories. These Meenies fabricated a fourth category and prevented performing artists from living in those apartments.

Twenty-five years later, when Manhattan Plaza was in negotiations with the new owners, Related Company, the tenants association and the policy committee never sought a vote by the tenants for their right of first refusal to negotiate for a condo conversion. These organizations even smothered the votes Susan Johann and I took, votes that revealed over 500 residents wished for a condo, non-eviction conversion, which would have relieved the taxpayers from their overwhelming yearly obligation and permanently secure Manhattan Plaza for performing artists. Instead, Related Company acquired double subsidies. So now taxpayers pay twice as much.

✳

REGARDING THOSE 169 section 8 contracts I have complained to every politician for thirty-some-odd years but never received response, from anyone other than President George W. Bush, because Eenies and Meenies bond well together. Laila Long and her husband moved into a two-bedroom apartment as a result of her complicity in re-allocating Section 8 apartments. By circa 1987 my continued objections finally forced Rodney Kirk and Lee Long to present documentation to prove what they had told our board in 1977, "The government sent us to make a correction by extracting 169 of the apartments away from the section 8 subsidies."

SAMPLE #1. Here is the complete document with its letterhead, circa 1988. This paper was a virtual confession, a document that revealed their lie. There never was any government that sent them to extract 169 contracts from this subsidy.

["The City of New York
DEPARTMENT OF HOUSING PRESERVATION DEVELOPMENT
Office of the Commissioner. Date: June 13, 1977

Departmental Memorandum
To: Files
From: Laila L. Long
Subject: Manhattan Plaza Board of Estimate Resolution

As part of the agenda of my meeting with Rodney Kirk this date, we discussed The Board of Estimate Resolution, which provides that Manhattan Plaza shall be rented in a ratio of 15% community, 15% elderly and 70% performing artists. The resolution did not include a specific provision indicating that the 10% fair market units were to be deducted before allocating units to the elderly, community and performing artists. The records are to be adjusted to indicate that in the future the total units to be allocated among the elderly, community and performing artists will be 1,520 units. The 10% (or 169) fair market units will be assigned separately.

Laila L. Long (her name was signed),
Assistant Commissioner, Equal Opportunity Division 111/gm"]

This note reveals corruption whether they actually wrote it in 1977 or whether they wrote it to provide the proof we demanded and dated it back to 1977. Throughout the past thirty-five years perhaps four hundred performing artists have been denied section 8 contracts so this is a significant fraud. A huge class action suit will be the legitimate outcome against them, the government and unions that enforced this lie.

Meenies are pragmatists. They know where, when, and how to cheat the system, regardless of how it affects others. They lurk for opportunities to grab the cash as the cow is shitting it. Once a subsidy has been established, jobs are provided and too often those who get these jobs pay no attention to the rules and regulations. This then becomes the ultimate corruption. Taxpayers pay for the subsidy and no one gives taxpayers a chance to opt out.

Approximately $385,000,000 has been contributed so far to provide this subsidy, which has been violated every day for the past thirty-six years.

SAMPLE # II.
[In 1977 Ruth Lerner, commissioner of HPD, responsible for this subsidy denied the request by the owners, before they actually erased the 169 apartments, to erase these 169 apartments. She stated, *"All 100 percent of the apartments have received Section 8 subsidies, and, in addition, performing artists who are rejected as tenants would have a right to sue."* They stole those apartments anyway.]

SAMPLE # III. Fortunately as I am writing this book, Eeney, meeney, miney, moe. . . . Catch a tiger by the toe. Here is proof these 169 contracts have been available all along.

["CB4 recommends replacement bus stop, prepares for water main project http://www.chelseanow.com/articles/2012/08/08/news/doc5022a038b21cb968374235.txt
Published: Wednesday, August 8, 2012 12:53 PM CDT
BY SAM SPOKONY
During the meetings public session, several members of an advisory committee at Manhattan Plaza a large residential building located at 400 and 484 West 43rd Street stepped up to the microphone in support of a letter from the CB4 Housing, Health and Human Services (HHHS) Committee to Related Management Company, the buildings owner. The letter signaled the committees approval of

Relateds recent proposal to transfer 169 units of Section 8 housing from Manhattan Plaza to a new building which is not yet built at 529 West 29th Street. Section 8 is an affordable housing program, which provides that no tenants in a certain building pay more than 30 percent of their income in rent.

Marisa, a member of the Manhattan Plaza Management Advisory Committee, added to her own positive remarks by reading a letter from the Manhattan Plaza Tenants Association. Related has proven to be a responsible and cooperative owner here at Manhattan Plaza, the letter noted. They have done much for our residents and have demonstrated a willingness to address our concerns at any time. We fully support this project. CB4s full board eventually approved the HHHS letter."]

Imagine the huge numbers now, after thirty-five years, of rejected performing artists as plaintiffs against the composite corruption of these Eeney, Meeney, Minney, Mo's: owners (both Aquarius and Related), government (both HUD and HPD), unions (MP Policy Management Committee), and the MP Tenant Association.

CHAPTER FOURTEEN

I RETURNED TO NEW YORK once *The Tavern* opened. I was very sad that its enormous success could have achieved so much more had Joe Stern and I been able to work with each other.

I found myself in true depression. I went to a Reiki therapist for a forty-minute session, during which time I slept. When I woke he was pacing and complaining, "Oh my God, my God, I can't believe it." I have often mused about the first moment after my death, and asked what he couldn't believe. He explained that there was only one word for what he experienced in the energies surrounding my body, and that word was goofy. Not the most flattering of words, especially if this really had been my first moment in Heaven.

"What," I asked, "is so goofy?"

"You have a brain that is so powerful you could do anything with it." Well, that sounded better than goofy.

"But every time my hands went over your heart, I have never felt such pain. You have a heart that has suffered greatly."

"I'm surprised you could find my heart. It's been shattered into so many pieces."

"Oh, it's there all right. And intact, but with great pain."

And I would agree. My friends think I'm more intellectual than emotional since I love to talk, debate, confront, evaluate, analyze, and conclude. I know, however, that first I feel deeply. Then I analyze those emotions. This is true also in my work. I feel for the characters long before I decide how to bring them to life. And in rehearsals I try to explore the feelings of those characters with the actors long before I worry about blocking, business, props, costumes, or any other externals. Most likely this results from a day in fifth grade elementary when my nun taught us to spell weltzschmerz and I discovered why I worry about people I don't even know. This has never left me. The Reiki therapist also discovered a hole in my right side. "Your energy stops here. Then begins again. There is a hole, right here." He pointed to the spot a young woman with crystals told me years earlier was karma, resulting from a lance into my groin as I rode on the front line of battle. The lance killed me, she said. Well, I guess it would. So I told this therapist, who was grateful for the information. He said karma would be the only explanation for such a break in my energy flow.

Three months later Joe and I met again in LA to receive *The Tavern*'s Outer Critics Circle Awards for Best Director and Best Production. This only reminded me how sad that Joe and I, two men who fit perfectly for the work, were still unable to work together. Why do we permit our petty frustrations to destroy the millions of good things that could happen otherwise? It is not so terrible that we are little boys, only that we cannot fulfill Wordsworth's "The child is father to the man."

There is so much about ourselves, as men in action, we do not know. God has provided many roads for answers, theatre being one, especially the classic plays. My life is most successful to me not just because I had a good career and loved it; or met wonderful people, including Don Linahan; or travelled and lived in my country, seeing everything firsthand. My life is most successful because my work helps me to know myself, to discover the ironies and paradoxes in my existence, and aim for bigger and better experiences. As I told my godson Johnny, "God will love you even more when he has more of you to love." Each of our vessels should be filled with as much of ourselves as possible before we return to God. But if we fill our vessel with dishonesties, each lie becomes the rotten apple that putrefies everything.

I am writing this book for the reader to find him or herself, as well as myself. Aunt Anna was right, "When you lose yourself, you lose everything." In today's society, it seems to me, just about everything presented to us is meant to make us feel bad about ourselves. When we go to the stadiums, we want to be Tom Brady; to the movies, Meryl Streep. On television any idiot who has a chance to show off in our living room becomes desirable. We are spectators, consumers, and fans, but rarely do we leave an event feeling better about ourselves. After all, we feel inadequate to those stars and their money. And the dramatization they create fails to take the creation deep enough for us to look away from them in order to view ourselves. In any society, it should be standard for those who create to inspire others to have more of themselves at the finish, like teachers who want their students to be brighter than they are. Recall Socrates to Plato to Aristotle.

Writing this book is demonstrating to me that as good as I wish to be, my choices were not always good, nor always right, nor always helpful. We all have work to do. After all, when I was in therapy I told Bernie Gertler, "Can you imagine how hard it must have been for Theresa to have me as a brother?" And with that realization I discovered why my sister was upset, at least part of the time. Theresa had troubles within her I did not have. Theresa felt cheated by life and assumed everyone gave me constant blessings and support. And though I do not believe that is how things occurred I certainly can see why she felt that way. I was a happy child who loved school, my friends, and the world. She wasn't and her moods were real. Then I failed to comfort my Aunt Anna because I could not face her death, so I wished her a Happy New Year and left her alone, minutes before she died.

I minimized so much of the good I accomplished at the union, at Manhattan Plaza, and in the regional theatre by walking away because I cannot tolerate corruption. I walked away from the O'Neill when Lloyd altered his code, away from my double casting success in LA because I could not trust Joe, from a full time job at Yale because the commercial spirit within that school lacked the spirit I believe is necessary in our art, and from the brotherhood of directors at SSDC because brotherhood to me is a high level of cooperation, discipline, and obedience to the common good, and they fail to have any of that. I fought to leave my past behind when I was a boy but in achieving that goal I left Theresa behind though I always stayed in touch. I relate to Tom Wingfield from Tennessee's *Glass Menagerie*, "Blow out your candles Laura, and so good night."

But as the years rolled by, the more of the world I confronted, the more of my family loomed in my psyche until I wrote *Brooklyn Odyssey* and re-ignited my love. My family was the only one I could return to because they were always available with the innocence of their love and food. "The world is too much with us," is William Wordsworth poem that so clearly reveals the pains and suffering we all experience. But, what other way is there? If we forfeit justice, truth, beauty and goodness only to be submissive to injustice, lies, betrayals and corruption does that not freeze us into a much lesser version of ourselves? I am convinced that succumbing to the evils of the world, even the tiny ones where we simply contribute just a little to get that something we don't deserve, but, oh what the hell, it is waiting for us to take it, winds up freezing us away from the warmth of our personal heart. So I do not feel it is worth giving up principles. I prefer the lonely suffering journey and the one that leads me towards the windmills of Don Quixote. He knew that his ideal world was not fantasy but, in fact, the true reality, which he would reach in eternity.

So, speaking for myself, the world does break your heart, but I would do it all over again.

✻

OVER A TWO YEAR PERIOD, prior to *Mixed Emotions* on Broadway and *The Tavern* in California, I was asked to direct *First Night*, a sweet, off-Broadway, two-character play. I turned it down both times because I thought New York critics would never support a heterosexual romance between two Catholic kids. And in view of directing *Mixed Emotions*, another romantic play, I felt it best I should be left out of this equation. You can get away with an occasional challenge to the critics, but it catches up on you.

However, while I was accepting my award in LA for *The Tavern*, I had dinner with Daniel McDonald and Jennifer Aniston. Daniel had been one of the actors in *The Tavern,* and the one most interested in my process as a director. Often he came to rehearsals that he was not involved in because he told me he liked watching my way of working with actors.

Because Daniel wanted to act in New York, and since I had twice turned down *First Night,* I asked him to read it, and I did the same with Julia McKenzie. Both said yes. So I accepted the job and returned to begin preparations.

※

BY THE TIME DANIEL MCDONALD moved to New York, I had received an emergency call from producers, who were eight days close upon an opening of Tennessee Williams's *Clothes for a Summer Hotel*, because their leading lady, Carrie Nye, leading man, and director had quit that afternoon. Apparently they had to quit because after three weeks of rehearsals, they simply could not fathom how to make the play work. So, lo and behold, the producers decided to ask me to take it over. I was, as usual, polite and professional but resistant, since I did not know the play, the producers, or the actors left behind in the production, and I certainly was not thrilled to have no time to create the unknown. But, being professional, I offered to read the script.

My witching hour is four fifteen a.m., so I woke to read this play. And loved it. It was clear to me why they had trouble, because the play is a ghost play. Everyone in it is dead. Being primarily mystical, I related. Early morning I agreed to direct it with Diane Kagan in Carrie Nye's role. Diane is pure theatre. She has tremendous talent and has dedicated an entire life to this work. Plus, Diane is as mystical as I am.

So I told the producers I would put together a totally fulfilled presentation but only as a staged reading. I could not spend time on sets. They agreed. I then hired Bobby Lupone, and we went into rehearsals with the leftover cast, who explained to me they had rambled on and on for three weeks with no rudder to their work. They apparently felt it necessary to make the audience understand they were dead, so they dedicated huge amounts of time to improvisations. They demonstrated to me how they entered spinning backwards in circles. I don't make this crap up! I told them that their characters were alive because they lived in the play, and besides none of these actors had ever been dead, so how would they know? Spinning backwards? How insane! Why not, I suggested, trust Tennessee? After all, Zelda and her aviator French lover dance in the middle of the play and speak in the present, future, and past tenses, so if by that point in the show the audience has not yet understood they were all dead, they would understand it then.

The producers tricked me by coming to rehearsal once and seeing such good work they secretly invited the critics, thus breaking their promise. Fortunately, unprepared as we were for that, especially Bobby who had a shit fit and believed I had lied to him about having no critics, the reviews were very good. Clive Barnes wrote about a dog named Lucky who finally found his true master, claiming that was what I did for this play, and he hoped someone would give me the chance to fulfill the show. Work long enough over the years as a freelance theatre director and finally I was compared to a dog named lucky.

Elliot Martin came to a matinee and asked me how I did it. He told me he produced it on Broadway with Geraldine Paige, directed by José Quintero and "Not one word worked." He also explained that in the first rehearsal Geraldine smacked José in the face, they never spoke again, and Tennessee went into complete silence. Well, no play can withstand all that.

Diane and I went into a state of abject depression when the show closed, speaking daily about the horrors of expectation as if we were once again young beginners learning the pangs of theatre. Perhaps this is what keeps us young, feeling betrayed always for the first time, the perennial experience and difficulty of letting go, moving on and hoping, despite the broken pieces, that your heart is still pumping blood.

❋

ONE WEEK PRIOR to the first day of rehearsals for *First Night,* Julia McKenzie got a pilot and decided not to come to New York to do the show. As usual, her LA agent could not understand my frenzy, since the pilot meant money and Julia fulfilling her promise only meant honor. Now I needed to replace one actor from the perfect cast in a two character play. The play is about a young couple who fell in love as kids. She became a nun for the past twenty years and he moons for her while going from one job to another. The play was well written, but I knew it would fail simply because it was not New York hip. Yet whenever I would discuss this with either of the two producers or the playwright, they would inevitably insist I was wrong because they saw it work perfectly in Boston. I was never able to make them understand the value that separates New York from Boston.

The play was crucified by the *Times* for being old-fashioned despite our satisfied customers. We ran for five months. Daniel McDonald benefitted the most. I was blamed by David Richards of the *New York Times*, who took potshots at me for bringing the show into New York, feeling that he had the right to do so because he and I played tennis together for two years. He felt "friendly" enough to attack me. How flattering!

But my spirit remained with *Clothes*. I regretted that Tennessee was not alive to be part of it. I felt I was aligned to his talents, and this production haunts me to this day because I believe it may be one of his greatest plays, though the original Broadway critics claimed it was his worst. How sad when the playwright is betrayed by those who cannot match his talents. Shakespeare suffers nightly throughout the world, as do Molière, Chekhov, the Greeks, et al.

※

SO, I RETURNED TO WRITING *Odyssey's* scenes of childhood, recalling my family during the war. How odd, the first thing I craved later in life, after suffering heartbreaks while rushing headlong into my future, was to return to my origins and take an objective look. I found myself in love with the family I had left behind and grateful for the power they imbued in me to be the brat it was necessary for me to be to travel beyond their fears. I saw that while they were frightened of life and of the American Dream, I wanted it badly enough even to abandon them, only for me to discover that the American Dream is the nightmare they predicted.

When I completed the screen version of *Brooklyn Odyssey*, which no one knew I was writing, I sent it first to Theresa. After all, her character is the most negative. She called minutes after she received it.

"I haven't read your book yet," she began, "But I did read the first three pages and I love the way you are writing this."

Thrilled and shocked, I was beside myself with her generous approval. Later that night she called again.

"Wow. What a great thing you have done. I loved reading this."

Being either brave or stupid I asked.

"What did you think of Theresa?"

In her usual frankness Theresa responded, "I think you got her right."

I could fly from then on. What a thrill to have the one character I created for her meanness compliment my accomplishment. The next day my father called and told me how fantastic it was for him to read the script and he wished my mother was alive to enjoy it. They were reading it as if it just happened. I had created a believability of their lives as if it was in the present. Extraordinary!

Theresa passed it on to Aunt Gracie, who lived blocks away from Theresa and my father, in Bethlehem, PA, at this point in the family's history.

"Anthony?'

"What, Aunt Gracie?"

"If Hollywood has any sense, they will give you the money to make *Brooklyn Odyssey* into a movie."

"From your mouth to God's ears Aunt Gracie!"

"You have brought us back to a time in America when there was innocence. Do you realize the generations that followed you don't know this existed, and through your writing they will learn that it was not that long ago. Something they need to find out now before it is too late."

Please bear in mind that none of them were readers, so their reactions were incredible. From this point on I just shoved one script at a time into the mail to all my friends across the states without warning. They were equally generous. Everyone was getting the same story. Since it was my first, I was learning about communicating with such a variety of people. Louis Smart, a black retired opera singer on my floor in New York told me after he read it, "Tony, I don't want to insult you, but you have written my story. Are you aware the same thing happens in black families?"

My story had the element I wished to create, universality. In *Brooklyn Odyssey* the boy winds up owning himself when he wins his battle to go for a classical education. Everyone needs to own him-or-her self be it in a wood shop, a bakery, marriage, farming, theatre, wherever.

So I braved postage to Vancouver, to my playwright friend Beverly Simmons. Beverly is artistic to the core, a nihilist, an atheist, and Jewish. After a long wait I called her.

"I was frightened when your script arrived, because though I love your work as a director, I feared I would hate your writing."

"What did you think about it?"

"I thought the writing was terrific, but I couldn't understand why you are so good to the church."

I knew exactly what she was getting at but wanted to force her to say it.

"What do you mean?"

"Well, you know."

"No, I don't."

"Sure you do."

"Tell me."

"Well, you read about it in the papers every day."

"Sex abuse?"

"Of course. Why have you not included any of that in your story?"

"Because my story is real, and none of that ever happened."

"Oh, come on, Tony, you're fooling yourself."

"None of that ever happened."

"Well, it was probably happening to other boys. You just weren't aware."

"Beverly, I was possibly the most active bridge between my classmates and the faculty. I was editor-in-chief of the yearbook, had my own offices and often stayed very late into the night. I was in numerous other clubs, as well as the horseback riding team, and the bowling league. I went to operas, movies, and plays with Jesuits. We played cards. If it were to happen to anyone, it would have been me. It never did." Beverly was stunned. So I asked again what she thought of the story, and now she said she was jealous. She would have loved such an environment. And her thought is on target, for the environment of Prep is exactly what our society needs now.

When JoAnn Robertozzi read the screenplay of *Brooklyn Odyssey*, she decided to gather an audience and have it read. I had met Zak Kostro by accident on a bus and discovered a young man of talent and good will, intelligence and heart. So I asked him to read the central character, which would normally be played by two separate but similar looking actors. But for the reading Zak read both Anthony, who becomes Tony, and read it so brilliantly that to this day when I have seen Zak and told him he is too old to play either Anthony or Tony on camera, Zak says, "Everyone says I look fourteen."

"But you wouldn't on camera."

"I don't care. I'm playing him."

How can you not love such an answer?

Eighty people arrived for the reading. As soon as it was over, two elderly women, who were not together but assumed I was the author, turned to where I was standing and asked if I knew how great a script it was. I said, "I am embarrassed to admit I've been thinking the same thing."

Then the audience forgot me completely and spent question-and-answer time talking about themselves, how they had conquered their odyssey or not, how they would do it now, and what they needed to proceed. I was thrilled. For my goal is to interest the reader in comparing points of my story to their personal life, adding, subtracting, agreeing, disagreeing, liking, hating, but always discovering that they have a story to tell. The more of us who take this step the further we will communicate universally.

CHAPTER FIFTEEN

ONCE MORE INTO THE BREACH! I was asked to judge plays in a festival in Dayton, Ohio, one July weekend. The festival was a yearly tradition at a community theatre. They treated the five of us, evaluators, wonderfully well. This festival had A+1 intelligence and attitude. It was one of the finest weekends I ever spent in theatre. These so-called amateurs managed over this one weekend to present three staged readings and three full-length productions on the same stage, followed in each case by full discussions between the audience and the evaluators with genuine interest in open questions that spanned form and content. And they served breakfast, lunch, and dinner in the lobby for everyone who attended each of the performances. How they found time to move one show in after another, including obligatory lighting and sound effects, I will never understand. Believe me, it is difficult to do what these people did and with such élan.

Several of their scripts were excellent. They asked the evaluators to read all six plays in advance and vote on them as soon as we arrived. Then at the end of the weekend, after the productions and discussions, we voted again. I chose *Asher's Command* both times as the #1 and it came in as the winner. But, of course, these people had no Eeny, Meeny, Minny, or Mo to obfuscate things because they were real people with full personalities, not clichés hiding behind each other. They were pure mid-western American citizens. They had faces, simple hearts and souls, a quest for truth, and fabulous buffets, ingredients for good theatre.

"Where there's a will, there's a way" was one of my mother's chants. Whenever I would act as if I couldn't accomplish something and needed help from her or someone else, she would challenge me with, "Where there's a will, there's a way" and make me do the thing for myself. I saw this clearly in Dayton. Unfortunately, in professional theatre, television, radio, unions, and housing, they find the wrong way because they have no will towards the right way.

※

Later that autumn Nicholas Nappi sent me his play about Cardinal Spellman and Bishop Sheen. I had already come to the conclusion that it was time for me to produce what I directed, and I was convinced the best theatres to present new plays were on Broadway. I spent hours in this pursuit every day. But because I do not come from a financial background, I had no bridge to the gold. This was not as devastating as it may seem. For one thing, I loved the overwhelming rewrites and that collaborative process, which was at its best at this point in my life. Nicholas was willing to fix every aspect of his script I could suggest, and I loved working the kinks of the script out with him. For another, I was once again facing reality about having no money and though it was brutal, it was reality. By the time I asked George C. Scott to read it, he was overwhelmed that it was so well structured and written, and signed a contract to star in it. He had called me at nine o'clock on a Monday morning despite the fact that he had only received it Friday, three days earlier. "I read the play two times this weekend because I was shocked there was a new play with a worthwhile plot and structure. I want to do it."

Not so easy once the Shuberts brought up Scott's drinking. Within the year of exhausting effort to overcome this obstacle, George developed problems with his legs and was no longer able to walk. I never wanted this word to get around, because I felt it would affect even his ability to find work in film or television, so I attempted no search to replace him for two years out of professional courtesy.

In time this magnificent actor died. What a loss to the theatre. I almost had the chance to direct him, as I had directed his former wife, Colleen Dewhurst.

※

A SPECIAL OPPORTUNITY OCCURRED for Jim Whitmore, Audra Lindley, and me to bring two full-length plays to New York on separate nights,

Handy Dandy and *About Time*, and perform them in repertory at the Houseman Theatre. What a great challenge! Repertory with two fabulous actors! But I had never been able to get rewrites from Bill Gibson for *Handy Dandy* and since I had invented a different set and an entirely new approach to the play in Pasadena from his original concept, my production of his play needed re-writes. Despite the success I had with my new concept, Bill refused to rewrite. But I had become adamant about his obligation to do so. So I called and told him I was coming to Stockbridge, Massachusetts, to his home and I would be there by nine o'clock Thursday morning. Bill told me he doubted the trip would be worth it. I asked directions to his house.

I arrived on time. Bill had written "Tony" and drawn arrows on some white 8x10 typing pages nailed into trees. The arrows pointed me up a hill to his writing shed, which like Bill was old, used, cold, and badly in need of a paint job.

For the first twenty minutes, Bill railed that he had "lost interest" in theatre. He "had no audience" and was now committed "only to novels." "My years of getting kicked in the balls by the critics are over and I am moving on. So thank you for coming, but sorry I can't help you. I warned you at least and I'm sorry for the trip you forced yourself to take."

I said not a word until it was clear he finished. Then I started.

"You're full of shit."

"What?"

"No one who doesn't care would write such incredible long speeches that dramatize the conflict between the eternal moral verities in existence for hundreds of thousands of years versus the legal jurisprudence in existence for only three thousand. So, don't try to persuade me you're not interested. You lost interest because when you wrote this play, it was agitprop theatre, the critics crucified you for it, and you're still burning. But I have changed all that and this play now lives and breathes as the play you want, but you need now to fix it to fit my production."

Moments after he recovered, he asked, "How do you want to go about doing this?"

"Page one."

Then, without either of us needing, hardly ever, to open the script, we spoke all day, except for a short lunch break in his house. I have never been more moved by a talent than I was that day, and I was confident with each request from me that his answer, "Okay, I got it," meant that the work would be accomplished the following day when I was gone. At about five p.m. we finished all my suggestions. We covered the script completely and had become friends. Bill asked, "Did you bring a tennis racket?"

"In the back of my car."

And we went to play for two hours on his court. When I drove back to New York, I did what I always do whenever I work with talents that prove God's existence. I pulled the car to the side of the road. And wept.

Bill Gibson heard truth that morning at his shed and rose to the occasion. I saw it. Every time I met one of those fully realized human beings, cranky or not, I was moved. In a man like Bill Gibson was the greatness needed to change this world, and if I was able to encourage him to step up to the plate again, then I too was helping to change the world: his, mine, ours.

And sure enough, handfuls of simple artists along with me do make this happen. I met and worked with so many hardworking artists who never achieved that gold ring Americans relish but who have the talent and generosity to create ensemble work that fortifies my belief in God. It is time to acknowledge the greatness of ordinary people in ordinary life, my mother, father, aunt Anna, journeymen actors, designers and crews.

※

AS SOON AS JEANNE DIXON'S prediction that I would fight enemies on a national scale and become blacklisted was fulfilled I was compelled to turn to new creative work. I then discovered how the new projects were best for me, creatively superior. I have a sixth sense that things from out of the blue are always worthy of my ongoing commitment. I sense that God is sending me a message, "Try this." Creativity is as essential as drinking water. Not-for-profit funding promised to become our prophet, to enlighten us. But if all we desired was commercial theatre, whether on Broadway or in Tuscaloosa why did America buy the lie? If truth is desirable we should hardly need an NEA. Writers write long before anyone knows they are writing. Kids draw, paint, dance, hum, do graffiti before being noticed. Dear Robert Frost, I hear you. Wouldn't it be nice fifty years after the creation of the NEA for an investigation as to how successful the program has been, or are we unwilling to seek that truth?

✳

OUT OF THE BLUE AS USUAL, Neil Thomas Proto, an attorney from D.C., contacted me to direct a concert in New Haven, his hometown, for the seventy-fifth anniversary of Sacco and Vanzetti's execution. There was a Dutch musical, called *Sacco and Vanzetti,* and Neil wanted some aspect of that music performed in some way. Would I take it on? Elliot Tiber, one of the Americans who adapted the musical into English lived in my building. So, we met and tried to create a collaboration, which in time turned out to be impossible. I did everything I could to find a way into this collaboration only to realize that Neil and I should abandon the project. When I called the Belgian contingent, I discovered that Dirk Brosse, the composer, and Frank Van Laecke, the librettist felt the same way.

"Tony, we thought you and Elliot were friends, so we didn't know what to say. But we do not want to continue with him. Would you and Neil take it over?"

"Do you have an English translation of your original work?" I asked.

"Only a poor literal one that was made when we performed in Dutch."

"Exactly what I want. Let me have it."

Dirk sent it. Neil and I would write out our sections and send them to each other for further corrections, until we completed our adaptation. What was most astonishing about this was that we shared so much in common, perhaps due to our Italian backgrounds. But, for me, the most interesting part of the journey was my discovery about Sacco and Vanzetti. In my attempt to decide what I felt about their innocence or guilt I researched their story and read opinions of their trial by people who lived at that time. And I learned the reasons for my family's fears. When my aunts, uncles and parents were children Sacco and Vanzetti, circa 1920 were captured, sentenced and by 1927 executed. This incident, coupled with the worse lynching in American history of eleven Italian immigrants in New Orleans, circa 1888 incubated huge fear into the working-class Italian Americans. How odd this was for me to begin to understand all my early orders, "Mind your p's and q's," "Our people mind our own business." Eventually we flew to Brussels to bring our copy to Dirk in his home in Ghent. He and Frank loved it, and we came to an agreement for our version, which we call *The American Dream*. We returned to the states to begin to find funds to produce a concert version of *The American Dream* at the Shubert Theatre in New Haven, several months hence.

※

WHEN I RETURNED to the United States I was scheduled to go into rehearsals with *Asher's Command* because after Dayton, Ohio, I had optioned *Asher's Command*. I had been submitting it to Broadway producers for approximately eighteen months, but they were not interested. So I found a way to bring *Asher's Command* to Sanibel Island. The playwright wanted to arrive without me as baggage, though I had spent nearly two years finding Sanibel Island to be a venue for this play and had weekly conversations with the Kennedy Center to arrange for their festival to have first rights if they chose at the end of the run on Sanibel. I was very busy making things happen for Marilyn and her play, but whenever I told her some Broadway producer turned it down, she blamed me for submitting it to that person. Marilyn had been academic, with documentary experience. She resented collaboration. This illustrates what happens when a person enters an industry without background.

I stayed with *Asher's Command* because I hoped to take it to the Gaza strip, because at this stage of my career theatre buildings and their problems were fading in my memory as the place I expect to find the kind of drama I crave. I stayed also because I made deals with the Kennedy Center and Sanibel Island, and I was obligated to fulfill my promises. But also, I was personally thrilled that my career was filled with world issues. *Asher* was about a mid-east crisis; developing Nicholas Nappi's play was about Cardinal Spellman and Bishop Sheen; Bill Gibson's *Handy Dandy* was about nuclear disarmament. I had already directed *Long Day's Journey Into Night* and found this play to be America's greatest play, because it was metaphorically the perfect reflection of America's problems today.

I gave the lead role of Asher, a young Israel soldier who becomes the general of the Israeli army over twenty years, all heart and soul, true milk and honey to Don Harvey. The result was complete transformation of Don from a gifted support, tough guy, to a valuable leading man. Nicholas Nappi saw the opening and told me at intermission, "A star is born." This was further proof that our work in theatre is as successful as the ingredients we put into it, like a great Italian sauce. Once we opened, Don said that in all his training he had never realized how easy this work really is. That is possibly because these acting schools want to get their money's worth and so they add, and add, and add layers of crap upon the obligation of the actor that does not pay off and was never necessary. I suspect that ninety percent of the great actors throughout Europe and America from the twenties, thirties, forties, and fifties knew virtually nothing about studying acting. They lived life.

Well, the Jewish community on Sanibel Island threatened to destroy the theatre if Schelhammer produced *Asher's Command*, because the play, though written by a Jew, had respect for the Palestinian mechanic, and such balance to that community in Sanibel was imbalance. But Robert produced the show. The result was fabulous. In addition to Don's performance, the cast and crew came together and the Kennedy Center arrived to award it a best play of the year. And the Jewish community experienced the humanity between the Palestinian and the Israeli and realized it was not some sociological and political put down of Jews. They were thrilled.

I took an enormous chance of casting Robert Schelhammer to play Samir the mechanic, despite big odds he could never do it. First of all, he is a political gay male who wants the world to know, which is why he wears cut-off shirts and short shorts. Then there are the earrings, attitude, and a very gay speech pattern. I even wondered how he was able to maintain his job with such externals. But after casting for two days, I knew I could not find the right Palestinian actor, so I asked Robert to audition for me.

I discovered he could really act. I don't mean this lightly. He had a range and a craft. I cast him and told him I planned to transform him into a Palestinian mechanic. For the first two weeks of rehearsal, I accepted Bob as he was and blocked the show, working the story with each of the actors and clearly established Don Harvey's spot as the centerpiece. But once all the foundation was in place, I went to work on Schelhammer, and every member of the cast was dumbfounded by the results. He became this strong, working class, Palestinian mechanic, father, husband, and friend to Asher. If I make myself sound like Svengali over Robert's transformation that is because I believe in that situation I was Svengali. So, let me have this much. At least I'm not claiming to be God.

I invited the Lark Theatre in New York to fly down to see the play, with the hope of bringing it to New York. Michael Chase Johnson flew down and loved it, but agreed with me that the first twenty minutes of act 2 needed rewriting. Marilyn was insulted that we would criticize what was by now an award-winning Kennedy Center play, plus one that had won over the Sanibel community, and had outstanding reviews for the play, my work, and the entire cast. This was a terrible turn of events since I continued to fantasize the Gaza Strip but the Lark explained that they had rushed to see the show because they wanted me more than the play and asked if I had any other show I could develop with them. They had a budget in place for something that could begin rehearsing in eight days.

CHAPTER SIXTEEN

WELL, I HAD *The American Dream*. So, with the insanity that is my signature, I agreed to start rehearsing *The American Dream* in eight days. Jim Sinclair was to be the conductor in New Haven but refused to become the musical director or participate in any way at the Lark. This necessitated that I find a musical director overnight, so I found Eugene Gwozdz, and together we found an entire cast within those eight days. I directed nights and went home to rewrite afterward, bringing new copy back to rehearsals regularly. During the days I began to produce the eventual performance scheduled for the Shubert Theatre in New Haven, which would occur three weeks following the last performance at the Lark Theatre.

Neil was in DC. I would either tell him what rewrites I was working on or ask him to add or subtract by email. Somehow we managed. Neil found the sponsors who, together with ticket sales, would have to pay $92,000 required for the Shubert concert. The concert meant bringing the entire cast to Connecticut for a week, as well as a full orchestra and full choral company, not to mention the costs to the theatre.

The American Dream was totally successful at the Lark and later at New Haven's Shubert. Dirk Brosse's music is as special as *Les Misérables*. Luckily Eugene Gwozdz was a fantastic musical director and had piano genius, so when he accompanied at The Lark it felt like a full orchestra. To this day I am grateful for this turn of events. I arranged the cast around the piano and isolated the two lead characters as they waited for their execution. Audiences not only loved the music, which I had predicted, but they loved the story, the characters, the songs, the staging, the cast, and the entire performance. They were moved by the show in a way I had not seen coming for they saw in it the horrors of injustice, though our adaptation leaned heavily on an America that still had hope.

Then I set out to bring the show and the entire company to New Haven for that one Saturday night concert version at the Shubert Theatre. I listed Jim Sinclair as the conductor and Eugene Gwozdz as the musical director. But two days before we arrived in New Haven, Jim Sinclair sent me an email at three thirty a.m., perhaps his witching time, demanding that he was not only the conductor but also the musical director and that I had to erase Eugene's name from the program. How odd, since he had refused to be the musical director and knew Eugene had done it, and therefore that work was already completed.

I must say that each time Jim Sinclair came into New York, the cast would question me. "Is that man capable of conducting this show? He seems like he's faking his reactions." When I called to explain why I could never list him as musical director, Sinclair insisted we would have no show unless I obeyed. You only need to meet me for five minutes to understand I will not do such things. With each of my attempts to save this issue that day, Sinclair seemed to feel he was gaining ground by making his intransigence more objectionable, assuming I was stuck and had no other choice but to cave in and agree to his insane demand.

So I fired him.

Every time something good is happening we fail because people like Marilyn Felt and Jim Sinclair have personal problems they never fix and when push comes to shove, they try to get away with something they do not deserve. Then I called Eugene Gwozdz and asked if he could conduct the show. When he told me he could, I called Orchestra New England, who Sinclair had called to tell them not to work for me, but they agreed to perform. I suspect they knew things about Jim I was learning. We only had Friday and Saturday in the theatre to rehearse on stage and, hopefully, sell tickets.

On Friday morning, Jim Sinclair had the *New Haven Register* print that he had been fired for no reason and that I was a monster. Not helpful for ticket sales since we had no other publicity except the notice of our performance. Sinclair is one of the worst people you can collaborate with, for so many reasons, but perhaps the worst is that he created chaos to free himself from public disgrace because he might not have had the talent to do what he claimed he could do. Being a conductor does not necessarily mean you can also be a musical director.

While Eugene struggled against time to walk through each of the sections of music, I roamed onstage to direct. We never exactly finished this rehearsal, though we came close, then broke to eat and dress quickly for performance. I introduced Mayor John De Stefano Jr. who welcomed the audience, then I introduced Rosa DeLauro, democratic Congresswoman who expressed gratitude for the opportunity to celebrate the lives of two Italian immigrants who were not given just trials. The audience was thrilled with the show. My cast was tremendous in their ability to sit through such difficult rehearsals, yet be able to perform fresh when called upon. Performers always save the day.

At the cocktail party after the performance Rosa DeLauro pointed to a man across the floor who told her he wanted to give me six million dollars towards Broadway but I keep refusing.

"Why, Tony?"

"Rosa, he says he needs two hundred thousand dollars, first, towards due diligence. Does that not sound like shit to you?"

Rosa agreed. This man and his partner from Las Vegas had been offering me several million dollars for each of my projects, but first I had to give them money. In my silly little idiotic brain I am smart enough to realize the scam. Six months later, I assumed they would call. "Tony we have good news and bad news. We were unable to raise the millions, but we only spent ($50,000.00) of your two hundred thousand so we can give you back $150,000. My response was always the same. "Bring the six million and I will take two hundred thousand off the top and give it to you." Corrupt businessmen prefer people who did not grow up in Brooklyn.

※

TWO DAYS AFTER the presentation in New Haven Massimo Mastruzzi, a young Italian whom I met in DC on one of my trips to raise money for *The American Dream* and who had come to New Haven for the performance at the Shubert, called from DC to ask me to write a musical about Cuba. I recognize the weirdness of this.

I explained I knew nothing about Cuba. I didn't write musicals. I didn't speak Spanish. I'd never been south of the border.

He accepted none of my excuses. Massimo Mastruzzi was from Rome but worked for the World Bank. He traveled regularly to Cuba and had a girlfriend there. He had composed dance songs that were appropriate for modern Cuba, and a Cuban, Abel Maceo Lemonte, had done the same with several other songs. And finally he found the code to crack my safe. "After what you did on that stage Saturday night for *The American Dream*, Tony, you can do anything."

I invited him to come to New York for Sunday dinner and play me his music. When he did, I found it sweet. These were songs but certainly not a score. I asked if he had a script. No, a libretto was what he wanted from me, and he had no parameters. Whatever I wanted to write about was fine with him as long as it weaved in and out of his and Abel's songs, a sizeable challenge I assure you, now that I've done it.

Once Massimo left I began to think. What do I feel about America and how might that contrast with Cuba? Never having been there, but having by this moment in my life traveled the United States ten times and back, and witnessed so much greed and general lack of ethics, I decided America has too much, Cuba too little. This was a great opportunity for me to create a story that reflected my complaints in our world. I didn't have any political investment in this matter. All I cared about was the notion of basic living. What happens to each country when there is too much easy living in America, and probably nothing but ongoing strain and struggle in the other.

So, I invented Maryanne, a Grace Kelly type of girl who lives in Ohio and whose father is a senator of the United States. Maryanne's life is perfect. She knows her entire future. Her destiny has been written for her. She knows the type of husband she will marry, where they will live, how they will raise their children, and how many children there will be whenever she returns home after lunch at the country club. So she feels stifled.

Her mother has recently died, and she asks her father to arrange for her to study dance in Havana. He does. Once Maryanne lands in Havana, she discovers poverty, filth, and struggle. But she also notices passion and women who dance from a place deep in their souls, and she envies their lives because they have to live day by day to find their destinies. Then, of course, she falls in love with Miguel, a Cuban singer.

Since Miguel's brother, Abel, is scheming to escape to America, their mother, Mamacita, is very upset that Miguel is now with Maryanne.

She believes this will also lead Miguel to flee to the United States. Maryanne's senator father is not happy to let his fellow senators know his daughter prefers the poverty of Cuba, so he sets out to force her to abandon her plan and return to her life of milk and honey. No one wants them to succeed. Their entire relationship is doomed from the start, so it is up to their power of love to free themselves. This aspect of my script turned out to be most interesting since it virtually condemned the Castro regime without my realizing it. My love of freedom simply entered into this script and was, in fact, the most political thing I could have created. I contacted our Treasury Department and discovered a professional permission for artists. Then I arranged a legal flight to Havana with all Cubans, and me.

❋

ONE MONTH PRIOR TO MY FLIGHT, I was in Portland, Maine, to direct *American Buffalo*. Rehearsals were magical and I suspect we found more than is usual about this well-written script. We were satisfied, as were the audiences and critics. Several days prior to opening I noticed a storefront on Congress Avenue with a billboard saying, "$15.00 for 15 minutes Horoscope Reading." Ahura Zachuur Diliizi, a Jamaican with blond dreadlocks, welcomed me in, sat across a table, and turned over the first three Tarot cards. He stared intensely at the cards and spoke without lifting his head.

"Within two or three weeks, you will receive an invitation to an exotic country to perform a difficult task you are nervous about. But if I were you, I would not be afraid because this is going to turn out to be a very important journey and one that will be very successful."

"Stop!" I yelled. "I am leaving in ten days for Cuba. How did you do this?"

"It's right here, though I did not know it was Cuba. But why are you worried? It will all work out, you'll see. You have been chosen from above and from here on you will work for them."

"Who?"

"Divine forces. They will give you renewed health because they plan to use you for a very long time till the rest of your life. You have had a busy time in theatre and you will continue to create, but from here on it will be more like missions that they send you to."

"I don't understand."

"They have witnessed your life and like the way you function. They now need you to do the same for them. In time you will see."

So we opened *American Buffalo*. My cast was tremendous and we were very proud of the work. My set designer, Leiko Fuseya, was splendid.

※

I FLEW DIRECTLY from Kennedy Airport to Havana. I had contacted the Treasury Department for a license and they showed me how to use their guidelines for professionals to travel to Cuba without breaking the laws. I did not want to sneak in or do anything untoward since my deepest motivation for going there and writing this script was giving a gift to the Cuban people. So I needed to be frank and honest.

※

ONCE THE PLANE LANDED in Havana and I found a cab, I went into a state of panic. When you have never been to a third-world country, but you've fantasized it from romantic pictures (thanks to the forties and fifties), it is difficult to witness the broken streets, the dilapidated housing, the dreary lack of color, no trees, no grass and certainly no flowers.

Massimo had given me a contact to rent a room, called a *casa particular*, in Centro Havana in one of the worst neighborhoods, but that is redundant. I arrived, after the depressing trip from the airport, and Abel was waiting to help me carry my luggage up the four flights of this tenement. Once we reached the top floor, I met Monica Leal and her mother, Melba who were my landlords, as well as Abel's wife, Janae. They were filled with that laughter Cubans generate daily for unknown reasons.

My room was neat and clean with a private, brand new bathroom, all white tiles. There was toilet paper, which I had been told would not exist in most of Cuba. Monica and Janae were both doctors around twenty-seven years old. After getting settled and visiting with them for about an hour, Abel suggested that he take me for a walk to the historic district to see the best of Havana. It was Sunday afternoon and we took the long walk along the Malecón. Abel was twenty-six years old at the time and had written half of the songs. Writing this script had been most difficult because the songs came first but also because I had to avoid political controversy. I had been informed that the Castro regime would eventually have to authorize it if it became ready for production of any kind. I had at least made the leading character want to embrace Cuba, which would be a plus to Fidel, though I did not do it for that reason since, frankly, it never dawned on me the project would go that far.

Abel spoke enough English to be helpful, and he gave me a tremendous insight into the history of Cuba. As we walked and talked, I began developing the deep emotions that remain in me to this day. It is painful to see a onetime beautiful island looking like a five-hundred-year-old farm lady, wrinkled and decayed. Ninety-nine percent of Cuba's ugly buildings brush shoulders with the few beautifully restored renovations by Cuba's commissioner, Eusebio Leal.

The police state was instantly obvious. Cuban police stopped us and demanded to see Abel's papers. I asked the first time what that was all about. Abel had to prove he was a registered music teacher and I was in Cuba to work with him on a music show. The police assumed he was hustling me, but easily accepted the truth once it was explained to them, but only after they saw his papers.

Commissioner Leal's work, wherever he has made improvements, is so beautiful it takes your breath away. You cannot help but cry for the lives of people forced to live within the adjoining devastated buildings. Genuine irony to view split images of ugliness choking beauty.

The next day, I walked and walked and walked by myself, unaware of the heat that crept upon me, filling my entire body with a temperature that took several hours that night to cool.

It was instantly clear that the sex trade was available.

"Amigo," girls in doorways would say as they winked you over.

Men would come right up to you and boldly point. "My room, up there."

I found myself checking everything from Maryanne's point of view. So my view of true poverty was incredibly mixed. I thought it was truly ugly and unbecoming as a way to live. I had great animosity for those Americans who make claim that Cuba is the right way of life; that Castro is superior to Bush; that Cuban education, medical benefits and just about everything else is better than ours. You have to be on heavy medication to believe such nonsense once you are there.

But mostly I was discovering the script I wrote was inadequate to the realities that now befell me. In New York, I had a romantic view without the right to such a vision. So, when Abel introduced me to Carlos Torrens, who would translate my script into Spanish, I insisted it wasn't good enough, though they both assured me it was very good. They were approving because they liked my basic plot, to have a girl from America see value in the desperate lives of Cubans. And I must admit that was the core genius of my script. But I had failed to know Cuba's tensions and the depressing lives, so I suggested I be left alone for two weeks while I studied Havana and rethought the script. Then we could meet and begin the translation.

First among many things I needed to accomplish was discovery of where and how to eat. There were no coffee shops, or any such conveniences. The Cubans have an open window occasionally on some first floors with a wooden board of bland homemade sandwiches. But in general, especially in the slums, shops are dirty and off-putting, and have little to no food. I was told that there was a dollar store if you had American money.

So, on my third morning in Cuba, I went to the dollar store and bought the few things available: two tiny cans of tuna, a small bag of dry biscuits, and two large bottles of seltzer. As I walked to the cashier, a young Cuban man in front of me was paying his bill, and when I was about fifteen inches behind him, his left shoulder literally shook. It was quite sufficient for me to realize he was reacting to me in some psychic way, and because I believed it was another sex trade, I turned left to the counter so I could look away from him. He then turned to look at me and wound up staring at my right profile. Then he told me.

"This is the year you will be blessed."

I was stunned.

"What?" As I turned to face him.

"You will receive a major blessing this year, and I wanted you to know that."

Then, he picked up his grocery bag.

I said, "Thank you."

He looked straight into my face and widened his smile from ear to ear as he said,

"Congratulations."

Then he turned away and left.

I felt I'd met an angel. I paid, then left the store and looked on the street but could not find him. I certainly wished to know more, but I never saw him again. However, from that moment on, the dirt and grime of Cuba was no longer in my way. Imagine, divine blessings first announced in Maine, now in Cuba, two weeks apart. For reasons I can never explain my view widened; my love of Cuba strengthened; my freedom on its dark, strange streets brightened. Cuba became a second home. I realized how my own background was humble, though far superior to Havana, but out of that humbleness I found the best values of my life. So I kept an eye and an ear (hard to listen when you do not speak the language) to the grindstone, and in time I did in fact discover that living without bling, Cubans have good souls. Many of them seem to live with innocence and gratitude.

I paid extra money to Melba for dinner and coffee with juice for breakfast. I walked without concern through as many side streets as I could to soak up the life of Cuba. I was so touched that I began to search for any church that was open, and wherever they held mass, I went. Eventually I found my favorite, though it was a good fifty-minute walk away, Cathedral Habana, in Plaza de Habana, a beautiful square and a great cathedral built by Jesuits two hundred years earlier. It had one of the most simple, elegant, and peaceful environments I have ever been in, mostly due to the gorgeous Cuban granite, soft grey with salmon woven through the stone.

I saw how much of a police state Cuba is because I was at the mercy of asking for directions wherever and whenever I went. Inevitably a Cuban cop would come between me and the Cuban I sought directions from. The officer would never speak, or offer help. He would simply lean his ear between us to try to understand what we were talking about. Once he realized it was not a sex hustle or some other illegal activity, he would simply slip away. Cuban police are there to protect strangers, but it is a police state nevertheless.

My life in Havana was improvised day by day. I had no plan, so I walked the entire city. My years as a New Yorker who loves to walk put me in good stead with my life among the ruins, especially now that I became familiar with it. I began to see the city from Maryanne's point of view, and nothing helped me to feel her desire to be like the Cubans more than the night I went with Abel, Janae, Melba, and Monica to the Garcia de Lorca opera house to see Alicia Alonso's ballet company perform *Cinderella*.

Abel got tickets, which cost a few Cuban cents. It was nighttime when we arrived, of course, and without streetlights, Havana is eerie. The Garcia de Lorca opera house is architecturally very elaborate. You know this is an opera house, but as with all of Cuba it is in terrible condition. If Havana looks like a wrinkled five hundred year old woman, the Garcia de Lorca looks like her twelfth husband.

First, I had to hide my face as we passed by the ticket taker for fear I would be detected as an American. Abel would have been blamed for buying me a Cuban ticket. Then we began the trek up the back staircase to find our seats. Well, without lights on the winding backstairs, I managed to fall twice, both times without the ability to see what I was falling against. On both occasions I came close to breaking each of my wrists as I held them ahead of me to break the fall. And believe me, my hands hurt.

We finally arrived at the highest point in the theatre, and our seats were in a tiny row directly above the stage. In fact, when I was able to get into my seat, it had absolutely no space for my legs, and I am not exaggerating. No space meant no space, not a little space. I had to climb above the seat, sit on it, and place my knees over the railing. I wanted to leave, but I didn't want to insult my hosts.

My head was so directly above the stage it was obvious I was not going to be able to see this ballet. Alicia Alonso arrived with her husband. Due to serendipity, the very first morning I was in Havana, I had been invited to meet Ms Alonso at a press conference, which I had done. I spoke to her that morning. She is tall and stately, and blind. Her husband helped her to find her way to the center box in the mezzanine. She received a standing ovation.

Lights dimmed. Music began. I took a breath and assumed I would have to hold it for two hours. Stage lights came on (rather low intensity). Cinderella was sweeping the stage. One second later, I fell in love. Truly. Her presence was startling. Alleyne Carena! Unlike most ballerinas, she was not only beautiful but also a fully rounded young woman. She had shape, breasts, hips, legs, a face, and a full head of Castilian black hair. She had character and immediately made me feel I was watching a performance that a great actress might create, a Gena Rowlands, an Anne Bancroft, any of our best. And possibly because she and the rest of the cast stood erect, I could see everything easily. Miracles were happening!

Alleyne established her character and when time came for her to dance, dance she did, brilliantly. The other characters were appropriately funny, two ugly daughters and a mother played by a man in drag. Because the show began so well, I not only forgot that I was hanging precariously over the balcony, but I wondered who the hell could possibly play the prince.

Then Romero Fromel leapt out from the wings, and I honestly felt I was looking into a book of fables. He was the Prince, personified.

But what is most astonishing in this story is how these two fell in love, appropriate to the script. They knew how to act in complete honesty. Alicia Alonso directed them superbly. Everything on that stage was real, available and appropriate. Their romance was occurring before my eyes. Near the end of the show, when dancers demonstrate their greatest talents, these two had the entire opera house screaming in joy. With every spin on her toes and his flight into air, we yelled breathlessly in unison. And I somehow never fell from that perched railing. Thus Cuba, artistic achievement surrounded by grotesque deterioration.

I wanted to fix my script to match that performance. But I had limits that made the rewrite very difficult. I had no desk, no computer, no lamp at night, no conveniences, and time was ticking. So I continued to roam the streets, crying quite often over the sadness before me. I would throw dark glasses on my face to cover my tears, but I was moved and it was profound. After all, I did not know anyone, so I wasn't crying over some specific friend or family member. When I was a child I could easily fill with tears over unknown people around the world suffering. And when I discovered through spelling class from Sister Raphael that the German name for these feelings was weltzschmerz I had a name for my childhood feelings. Now I was discovering that Cuba was the place that I had been empathizing over throughout my life. I was finally experiencing weltzschmerz firsthand.

One hot day I decided to visit the Karl Marx Theatre. I heard it was very large, modern and far away in Miramar. But I had not counted on how far away in the heat of that day. So I walked toward the angle I assumed I would find it, and with the help of my dictionary asked numerous Cubans along the way who spoke no English, "Karl Marx Theatre?"

They would respond with horror.

"No aqui."

"Si pero donde?"

"Lejos esa manera."

"Far that way" was accompanied by pointing in the direction. Several hours later, I arrived and looked frightening enough to worry the women who managed the theatre. They brought me a towel and bottled water. Nothing could erase the sunburn. I was a walking lobster. I explained the purpose of my visit as an American director writing a script for Cuba, and they took me around their beautiful Karl Marx theatre, the most well kept in Cuba.

As I was leaving, they tried to call me a cab, but walking was on my mind and I wanted to return on foot. I took a separate route this time, along the Malecón, and three quarters of the way home, I stopped at the Hotel Nacional in the Vedado district. I had been there one afternoon and knew they had a beautiful lawn overlooking the ocean, so I found a shady tree and slept beneath it for a half hour. Then I continued to Zanja y Hospital where I lived. When Melba and Monica heard what I had done, they laughed for hours and wondered what kind of crazy person was renting from them. But walking has always connected me to people's lives, and this is what I needed more than anything else to finish the script. Plus this walk proved the inequalities within a socialist state, for the neighborhood in Miramar was comprised of those 1930s homes built as the Beverly Hills of Cuba. This is where ambassadors live, and of course, high-ranking members of the regime.

So I added tensions to the script. Before Maryanne arrives in Cuba

Miguel is already breaking away from his girlfriend Caridad, but once Caridad learns of his interest in Maryanne Caridad sets out to kill Maryanne. Charles, Maryanne's father, arrives unexpectedly to persuade her to return with him. He stays at the Hotel Nacional. And Abel, Miguel's brother, escapes the island with friends on a balsa, which frightens Mamacita that Miguel will do the same. Finally, with all odds against them Maryanne and Miguel realize they are free to love each other and they also realize that their love provided personal strength to withstand the slings and arrows enveloping them. They know their freedom for love is stronger than everyone else's attempt to stop them. This theme of freedom by itself was enough to become a strike against the regime though I was not yet aware of this.

I then spent two full days with Carlos Torrens while he translated as I spoke and Abel watched. A few days later I returned to New York, reborn. Friends asked how I had traveled to Cuba without the slightest knowledge or awareness of what the hell I was doing. I couldn't answer except to suggest that my freelance, independent career prepared me perfectly for this unique journey, but more truthfully, I think Zachuur, the astrologer in Maine, and the Cuban I met at the grocery knew the answer: "This is the year you will be blessed." People are the same the world over. It takes time to notice distinctions and similarities. Cuba has good people like my family and friends but it also has Eenies, Meenies, Minies and Mos.

※

MINIES emerge as the prototype of people who neither grab the gold ring as the Eenies do, nor openly wait in the wings to take over as the Meenies do. The Minies are the vast populace who take advantage of any mess without any desire to clean it up. They feel comfortable to hide where they can hope to receive something more than they deserve. They believe they don't have talent or power to deserve anything and they lack a personal knowledge of how to survive on their own. They are the "What, me worry?" crowd. They are scared to death of life.

For instance, whenever I inform fellow tenants at Manhattan Plaza about how the taxpayers are being cheated while we live in comforts paid for by them, a glaze comes over their eyes as they usually say, "So what Tony? We deserve it." Therefore it doesn't matter to them that people are being cheated to provide for these Minies. At the union, the majority of directors are out of work the majority of time, so just the idea that some day they'll have a show to direct is sufficient to their needs. The SSDC could kill people for all they care, and how illegitimately the SSDC was formed or how it managed a monopoly over other unsuspecting directors is of no concern to them. For them, a union is a big daddy fighting for their rights, so if ever they are hired to direct a show, all their dreams will come true. These are paradoxical farces in the making! At Actors Equity they tell seventy thousand out-of-work actors they're not allowed to work unless they have a union contract. But ninety-five percent of them do not get union contracts, so the union insists they cannot work. Can you imagine such stupidity? Why not tell one hundred percent of your actors, "Go to work, wherever, whenever you can. Gather other talents and put on a show in the school, the fire department, on the street for God's sake, but work, create, demonstrate your God given gifts. Then, in the event your show develops commercial viability, come to us and we will help you create the contract." But no, actors prefer to dream that their union is right and will help them and this is what creates such impotence among actors who avoid life and the world in the process.

Minies weave their way through your life with the excuse that they're required to "sell out" to survive. They'll use any means to get ahead. The worst of their qualities though is their willingness to exchange love. This turns out to be false affection to induce your aid. Minies put their talons into your heart and make you feel wonderful while they act as your best friend, lover or collaborator so you don't notice that they're sucking the life out of you to get what they want.

In spite of wounds I suffer from Minies' greed to get ahead, or their deceit that breaks my heart this too has caused me to know myself. For Minies see our limitations before we do, and this is why they can take such advantage of us. Then, when we're bleeding and weeping to lick our wounds, we can either waste our time complaining or investigate and see ourselves as they saw us. For instance, when a Miney tells you for twenty-five years how valuable you are and how the thousands of conversations have helped him see more clearly truths previously hidden, you assume you have developed a friend and that together you now have a friendship you can depend upon for the rest of your life. Until that day when that Miney says, "I just got in touch with my true feelings and I hate every conversation, interpretation, evaluation, analysis, and conclusion we ever had for the past twenty-five years." With a snap of a finger a Miney is able to lie, either about getting in touch with their true feelings, or the twenty-five years they faked the lie that made you believe in the lasting friendship. In that snap of a finger, a Miney can alter everything instantly, leaving behind nothing of any gratitude concerning you. And they can do this because the twenty-five years were only about them. You never really existed as far as they're concerned. You facilitated all kinds of things they enjoyed. But, you caused them to come to some conclusion about themselves, which they are now too frightened to accept so they see you as the cause of their fear. Now you must be thrown out with the bathwater so that not one iota of those twenty-five years ever existed. A Miney lives without conscience to remain in a state of readiness for escape. And for them, the best preparation for escape is to activate fake love.

Our country is packed like sardines with Eenies, Meenies, Minies, and Mo's. They live among good people in every one of our relationships, and, sorry to say, it is difficult to detect them because they look like us, act like us, and need us as much as we need them. The only difference is their readiness to destroy.

In every profession, every bureaucracy, every neighborhood, we have Eenies, Meenies, Minies, and Mo's. It is urgent we start recognizing them as part of the art of men acting before everything good gets destroyed.

✻

I RETURNED to Portland to direct *Lion in Winter* and I visited Zacchuur.
"How was Cuba?"
"You remember me?"
"Of course!"
"Well you were right on. Cuba was tremendous and very special."
"Let's do another reading," as Zacchuur placed several Tarot cards on the table, then told me.

"You have to go back."

"Where?"

"Cuba. She needs you."

"Who needs me?"

"Cuba."

"What do you mean?"

"You will do something very important for the Cuban people. They need you to go and do this.

"Zacchuur, if my friends hear that an entire country needs me, I'll be a dead man."

"But it's true. Cuba does need you, and you will provide something good for them."

"How do I go back?"

"Those arrangements are being made now. You have no need to be concerned about them. Just go when the time comes."

After *Lion* opened I went back to New York.

※

WHILE WAITING UPON CUBA, an opportunity presented itself for Jim Whitmore, Audra Lindley and I to remount Tom Cole's *About Time* in Victoria, on Vancouver Island. And what a treat that was. First of all, the setting is beautiful. Victoria is the capital and filled with wonderful craft shops run by very talented young people. They display totem poles, masks, knit goods, leatherworks, pottery, and every inventive product that is a delight for the eye to behold. Then there is the view of the state of Washington across the waters from a park embankment. We lived in a tremendous hotel on Victoria's gorgeous wharf. We each had suites, with two bedrooms, kitchens, dining and living rooms, two bathrooms, and two terraces. Could have lived there for the rest of my life.

I directed *About Time* in a Pantages Theatre, now called McPherson Playhouse. It was British to the core and so elegant in its black and white environment, the perfect proscenium theatre with fabulous sightlines and acoustics. And a great British crew of real professionals! We opened Tom's play to a fabulous audience and thrilling reviews.

I had hoped to vacation afterward by driving the west coast of Vancouver Island, which I was told was mostly desolate and beautiful on the way to Alaska. But the night we opened it snowed, and this otherwise warm island was ill equipped to rid itself of just a few inches of snow, so I changed my plans and took the huge ferry to Vancouver through that wonderful clump of San Juan Islands. In Vancouver I stayed with Beverly Simons and had meals with her and her three very educated sons. When one thing doesn't work out, something else does. You just have to learn to accept the good with the bad.

CHAPTER SEVENTEEN

CUBA WAS ON AGAIN. Massimo had used a great deal of energy to make this happen. Because he is Italian, he has a European passport, so he can travel in and out of Cuba. Massimo spoke Spanish, so he had that convenience as well. He found the method to move forward with a production as long as I would return without him and direct my script in a language I did not speak. Massimo would continue to be in DC making a living while I would be suffering the poverty of Cuba, my usual partnership.

The Compañía Danza de Nacional Contemporánea, famous in Havana for modern dance, read the script and requested that I go there for three months because things in Cuba move slowly (truthfully they do not move at all) to direct *Habana Carnaval* with their dance company. How could I refuse such a great opportunity? Massimo had created a miracle. Plus Zacchuur insisted I had to help Cuba, grandiosity right up my alley.

So, of course I began to make arrangements. The timing of everything in Cuba is difficult because to them a starting date can be next week, next month, next year. They aren't going anywhere, so there's no reason to be forced into the anxiety of a calendar. From my end I had no clue as to how to begin this process, or who these people were, or what would happen once I arrived. Perfect challenge for my career! Plus I needed to remain free of American work to be available to travel to Cuba in a flash. A costly problem at best!

During preparations several months passed and dates altered continually while I shuffled with issues at home. For one thing, my legs went dead, from the top of my thigh, right at the joint of my hip, down to my ankles. Dead! Neither of them had any life left. They felt like sand bags, and caused me to walk inch by inch. Numerous friends dared bring up my age as a possible excuse, but I would have none of that.

After all, my legs have always been strong and useful, and though this deadness occurred overnight I could not believe it was intended to remain. Actually, from the day this problem began until its termination, I suffered for fourteen months. Then, prior to my trip to Cuba, my left knee broke in some way I could not fathom.

A Cuban neighbor of mine in New York was fascinated that I had gone to Cuba, survived and was about to return. He told me that he and several friends were trying to get some important documents to a family in Las Tunas.

"Let me have the papers. I will bring them to this family."

My neighbor was horrified.

"Tony, you could get into a great deal of trouble. This is a family who were attacked by their neighbors because they complained that Castro had jailed their father because of the Varela document several years ago. The neighbors broke the back of the eighty year old grandmother."

I had been aware of the Varela document from my first trip to Cuba two years earlier. Seventy-five activists were imprisoned for seeking rights from the Castro regime. Inconvenient freedoms people thirst for! How dare they.

So I told my friend I would take the chance.

"You do not know what can happen to you if you were caught."

"In fact, I do know but if these people are in such need, and I am going there why not take the chance?"

He knew I was serious so he refused to tell me more.

Finally my plans were made to leave New York. As I was packing, Don Linahan called and was very upset. Don was the godfather of my niece's oldest son, Michael, and had just finished a bad phone call with Michael's mother. Don said that my niece claims she and her husband use tough love on Michael, but based on her mean tone tough love and tough shit are synonyms.

"I almost yelled at her. She was so negative about Michael."

"Why didn't you?"

"Well, I wasn't sure I should."

"You're Michael's godfather Don. Doesn't that give you an obligation to fight for him?"

"Well, I am sorry now that I left everything to Evelyn in my will."

"Frankly, when you told me you were doing that a year ago, I was shocked."

"Really? Why didn't you say so?"

"You never asked my opinion."

"What should I have done?"

"Why leave your savings to the mother who has no love of your godson."

"Who should I leave it to?"

"Michael, your godson!"

"But Michael is constantly fucking up."

"So then you're the perfect godfather, a fellow-fuck up! This might help Michael pull himself together. I doubt you have very much money in any case, but this would boost him to know someone believes in him."

"But Evelyn is the executor of the will."

"Look, Don, if you want to change your will, change it. That is your right."

"I think I will."

And so I left for Cuba. I tried to get through the airport with three huge duffle bags and about eight smaller shoulder bags with straps choking my neck.

"You can't bring all that onto the plane without paying extra, and we need to weigh it. It'll come to a couple of hundred dollars."

"But I'll be in Cuba for three months. I need all this."

"That's your business. Just pay for it."

An airport angel appeared. "Excuse me. You are going to Cuba?"

"Yes."

"Okay," she said to the others. "I'll take care of him."

She then came around to the front of her counter, took two of my bags and led the way. We were late and had to move fast. So I dragged my dead legs as I went, slowing her up.

"How come you're going to Cuba?"

"I've written a musical. I'm going there to develop it further."

"That's wonderful. Good luck with it."

"How come you're helping me?"

"I'm Cuban."

God is my co-pilot. She was unflappable to guards along the way who tried to stop her.

"It's okay. He's going to Cuba."

She had a way of making it sound as if I was defending America and all my weapons were in my shoulder bags.

I asked her, "Do you ever go back?"

"Once I got out, I never wanted to return."

Then she shouted ahead to someone holding the door to the inside runway, "This guy is going to Cuba. Don't close the door." I never got the chance to get her name to send her anything, but she looms in my memory.

That night in Havana, Monica Leal waited with a cab driver five hours for me in another part of the airport after my plane landed. At immigration I had to go through a young Cuban who interrogated me through the ugly booth he sat in while I stood foolishly above him trying to communicate without the ability of language. He interrogated me slowly as if he doubted everything I said. I gave him the address of the *casa particular* where I would be living, with the names and telephone number of my landlords. I gave him the name of the Compañía Danza de Nacional Contemporánea and address where I would be working. He checked something I could not see below the counter upon hearing each bit of information. Perhaps he was checking a telephone directory, if such a thing even exists in Cuba. Fortunately, everything I told him was true.

I was unable to make him understand that I was legitimate, that I was here to direct my musical. He took a beat, then looked with anger into my eyes.

"You come to a third world country to work?"

Well, shut my mouth, what a clever question.

"It is not exactly work. More like a gift."

He just stared waiting for me to add something that made sense to him.

"I am not being paid."

So he let me pass.

No one ever leaves Cuba with Fidel's money.

The real trouble began in customs. They kept me for five hours without telling me why. They held one of my large bags, but they did send me back two other duffle bags, and of course I still had my eight cloth bags that had been wrapped around my neck.

The duffle bag they held back was filled with about five hundred dollars' worth of gifts, which I brought for the Cubans who were now friends. And it included one cheap desk lamp, so I could see at night in case I wanted to fix my script at the end of the day, though I never did have such energy. Eventually they brought me into the customs section and without a smile from any of them, indicated for me to open the bag and dump all its contents onto the table.

They were stunned to find one huge ball of 100 percent cotton, which I was bringing for the women to make dresses for themselves with all the necessary threads, needles, and trim to complete the job. This caused the angry female officer to bring several others over to check it out, and though it was wrapped in plastic, they never insisted I cut it open, nor did they even speak to me at all. The rest of the bag had several recorder machines for taping messages. I wanted Abel to have one and my translator, Carlos Torrens, the other. I also had about two hundred dollars' worth of chocolates for Melba, a candy freak. The lamp apparently had been detected in x-ray as a possible weapon. If you could only see their eyes as they realized how this silly cheap broken lamp had caused such consternation, but being efficient Cuban police types, they revealed nothing in their expressions. I, on the other hand, had irritation oozing out of my pores.

Monica was faithfully waiting with the taxi driver who was earning twenty dollars from me. It was worth his while since twenty dollars is a fourth of a year's work for the average doctor in Cuba, like Monica. This time I did not need to acclimate myself to Havana or to my surroundings. I had done that two years earlier. But I now had problems walking, and the place I was living was still up four flights of a dirty tenement and the place I was working was two miles down the road. For an American, cabs in Havana are the same prices as New York. You are not permitted to ride in Cuban cabs, only in Fidel's state tourist taxis. And I was warned never to get on one of those ugly buses the Russians built. They were dirty and filled with pickpockets.

So I left forty minutes early and walked to work and back again, assuming the exercise might bring my legs back to life. As for the knee, it remained swollen the three months of my license. I iced it every evening to ease the pain from bags of water I froze daily in the small refrigerator in my room. At the dance studios, which were across the street from the headquarters of the Cuban government and across an open field from the *Plaza de la Revolución*, the dancers had a room for therapy and the Cuban woman who worked there used every cure known by her. She even used some sort of burning cigar, an African treatment, but nothing ever stopped the swelling.

When I met the managers of the Danza Co. who were to become the producers of my musical, they introduced themselves: the choreographer, the designer for sets and costumes, and believe me there is a God, the tremendous Laura Roman Romillo, my translator. No one had prepared for my arrival. They figured I might never arrive, so unless I did they would lay low. Then there was a money problem. Because I was from America, the Treasury Department only provided guidelines to do this job as long as I did not engage in commerce with Cuba, no money to me, no money to them. Massimo knew the rules I was obligated to follow, and I knew Massimo and several of his Italian friends were raising money so we could take what I did in Cuba on to Venezuela, Costa Rica, Spain, or Italy. They told me they hoped to raise $100,000 for the tour, which would even include the United States if we could get visas for the cast to travel to America. I offered to seek that help from President Bush.

I had production meetings with my collaborators in a small office. There were six of them, Laura, and me. To begin, we had to discuss dates and the procedure to move forward. I had to speak to six Cubans, and they had to respond while Laura translated them to me in English and me to them in Spanish. It was a six-ring circus, and I would leave these exhausting meetings with tremendous respect for Laura, who almost never missed a beat, but when she did, she had the confidence to stop us so we could repeat whatever was confusing her. Weeks later at press conferences, Laura would jokingly get me to slow down. We were friends from beginning to end. Laura was twenty-two years old. Fantastic.

Then my collaborators informed me the show was cast. Wow! "No way, baby," was my response. What do you mean the show is cast? I haven't auditioned anyone, so how could the show be cast. Well, Cubans have a fear of authority, I guess because they bow down to a dictator and assume whoever is the authority is also the dictator, so they immediately answered, "Of course, we mean cast only until you audition them, Maestro." Maestro was a title I found off-putting as an American. But they were quite sincere in their use of it.

So I auditioned the members of the dance company and discovered that none of them could sing or act. Cuba had not produced a musical since Castro took over, forty-eight years earlier. Musical extravaganzas, yes, but no book for fear something might slip into the dialogue that would be objectionable. So, Cubans never trained to do what Americans train for: sing, dance, and act all in one.

What to do? My collaborators suggested that we only use scenes for the dancing. Typical Cuban solution! Run away! After forty-eight years of submission to a dictator, only he has testosterone. Theirs dried up with the right of free expression.

"We are doing the entire show," I boldly announced. Though, admittedly, I had no idea how. When I direct in America, I always have some secret actor or designer I'm aware of who can help me. In Cuba, I had no sense of how one even finds other talents. But I demanded that they search for someone who could at least sing Maryanne and Miguel, as well as Mamacita and Charles, Maryanne's father.

As written, Maryanne was the Grace Kelly of Ohio, but try to find a Grace Kelly in Cuba. So, they brought me Gretel de la Oca, who was a dancer from another company and could act. I really liked her quality though she was obviously Cuban. Being the author, I was wise enough to realize all I had to do was alter my script and accommodate the idea of casting Gretel as a Cuban American. I was so busy making this adjustment I failed to notice that she couldn't sing. Plus, Demetri Monez, my musical director, was away in Santo Domingo during the week of auditions, so I had to try people out without musical accompaniment. But I was grateful to find Gretel. I rewrote the father, Charles, to be one of the original young Cubans permitted to leave Cuba with the Pedro Pan exodus back in the seventies. And, now I would be able to cast a

Cuban to play Charles. And as his main song at the end of act 2 was basically opera, I would need a Cuban who could sing opera.

For the male love interest, Miguel, they found me a Cuban with a beautiful voice, Carmelo. He was right every way except he was softer than Miguel should be. But again, I was grateful. After all, I believed I was experimenting with this material to give the Cubans the gift of learning about a full-fledged type of musical and only hoping we could tour and develop it outside of Cuba.

I found a good type for Mamacita and though she could not sing she was very much the mother, so I cast her. I tried numerous people for Charles until they brought me Pedro, a six-foot-four black opera singer built with the stiffness of a totem pole. He was from one of the opera companies and I was thrilled. However, my Cuban collaborators took me aside.

"No, Tony, no Pedro por papa."

"Porque?"

"Pedro es negro," pointing to the dark of my pants.

"Si, tan que?"

Again with the indication on my arm, *"Gretel es blanca."*

Blow me down, they could not conceive of a black man as a white girl's father.

?!?!Cuba?!?!

So, I told Laura to tell them to visit my building in New York where white and black are often related. And I cast Pedro, though his stiffness was so overwhelming I kept blocking him in a chair to divide his height into two parts. Around this time I felt like I was starring in a British farce, *Peter Sellers Saves Cuba*. I had been there for several weeks. But I could sense my collaborators were not yet working on anything. So, I called a production meeting and discovered they were waiting for money from Massimo and his friends.

"What money?"

Talk about being the stupid American!

Laura explained, "Massimo promised to give them money for the costumes and set. They can't begin without the materials."

I had no way to call Massimo, but because he worked for the World

Bank in DC, he was able to call, if we could arrange for me to be by a phone. Somehow we had that first conversation.

"They say you're giving them money for materials."

"I promised them some of the money we're raising for the tour."

"You told them you were raising money for the tour?"

"Yes."

"How are you bringing this money?"

As he began to tell me, I realized I was now on the verge of trouble and caught inside a situation I could not resolve. I simply said, "Never mind, I shouldn't even know. Just let me know when you're arriving to do this. It's holding everything up."

How easily we become criminals.

Once you tell a Cuban there's money, trust me, it is all they hear from that moment on. Every store in Havana, every hustler or whore on the street sees dollars in your pocket as if you are wearing white cotton see through shorts, soaking wet to reveal US dollars. When I would brag to Melba and Monica that the hustlers and prostitutes were always offering themselves to me they would laugh and say, *"Usted sabe,* Tony, *no est'a sobre amor."* Indeed it's not about love, but I knew that.

So, I told my collaborators to sketch sets and costumes while I would use the dance studio to show the cast how to learn to deal with blocking. The room was large, modern, and surrounded by windows that looked out toward the *Plaza de la Revolución*. There were folding chairs and one very long ballet bar, mirrors on one wall. Unfortunately, there was a parallel dance studio directly below with loud bongo drums during all our rehearsals, so in addition to all other discomforts, I could not even hear them speak the language I did not understand. Might as well be directing puppets, Kukla, Fran and Ollie.

I started teaching Acting 101. First of all, most Cubans speed-speak. Some of them cannot even understand each other. And clearly I could not understand anyone. So I turned this to my advantage. If you give two Cubans a three-minute scene, they will speak through it in fifteen seconds. So, because the musical opens with Miguel and Caridad, in bed, I took the two actors and told them to lie on the floor as if in a bed. Then I explained that Miguel's pants would be upstage of the bed, so when the lights came up he would with frustration push himself off of Caridad, spin his body with his back to the audience, and put his pants on. Then, I told Caridad to ask, after it is clear that she is surprised by this turn of events, "*Que pasa*, Miguel?"

When we tried it, they rushed, so I asked them to react before speaking. Think, why, for instance, why is he angry enough to break away, before you say, "*Que pasa*, Miguel?" Wait for an answer. When he doesn't answer, repeat with more urgency, "*Que pasa*, Miguel?" At this point, Miguel, now in his pants, could turn to her with disdain and say in Spanish, "You know what's wrong," then cross to the front of the bed to put his shoes on while Caridad rises on her knees, covering her nakedness with her blanket, and tells him she has no idea what he's talking about. Now he sits on the edge of the bed to put on his shoes and tells her he knows she has been sleeping with *extranjeros*, tourists, and he is now breaking off from her. I was showing them how to take the time to create stage reality.

Caridad physically then holds him back as he rises. She tells him that sex with strangers is just business. He must understand. It doesn't mean anything. I told Miguel to make certain, in character, that he fully takes in her foolish answer, realizing he could never trust her again, then make a break for it, showing in his body he is finished with her. She clearly gets the point and threatens him that she'll never let him go.

I was showing the cast that dialogue is supported by action; how to project and to send out the point of each scene.

For the nightclub scenes, where Abel, Miguel's brother, performs as emcee and singer, and Caridad and her brother Pupi dance, in traditional Cuban fashion, I simply arranged the rehearsal room's ballet bar onto a diagonal angle across the room, put two stools on one side, and told the actor playing the bartender to pantomime making and selling drinks. Then I showed the remaining cast where to sit at nightclub tables before, during, and after dancing in the first scene, in which Maryanne arrives and meets Miguel. It was all so primitive. Returning to ground zero in my work after years of great collaborations in America was a test I had not expected to take. But clearly I was in my element. Rehearsal is where I belong no matter the circumstances.

In this third week, I told the designers to come to see how the show could look from one scene to another in a skeletal manner. They could then think about what they needed to do. I assumed it would be a mess, but figured we were just trying to get started and it would cause all of us to become joined in three-dimensional terms.

My collaborators arrived, and the cast began to demonstrate what we had done to date while I stood, watched, and wept for joy! These kids, mostly around twenty-two years old, were so touching, so professional, so without guile, so faithful, so capable of retaining all the work without our ever having repeated it as the week progressed. And I never saw a script in their hands.

My weeping never ceased. During the next two months of rehearsals, I cried and cried, shamelessly. I had come to Cuba to offer a gift, and they gave me the best one instead, showing me how, once again, heart and soul is mostly all that is required. Possibly the best pill we could ever take is a rehearsal period that is blessed. Everything to me becomes an emblem for life itself, so whenever I find innocence I recognize how our world is failing by trying to live without innocence.

However, the singing was further held up because once Demitri returned from Santo Domingo, he never came to rehearsal, arguing that he had to orchestrate all the music on his broken computer system at home.

I had left Melba and Monica's phone number with a friend in New York in case of emergency and was called late one night to discover that Don Linahan had died in his apartment, having fallen against a wall with a slash on his head. Of course, there was no way I could return to attend a funeral. I might as well have been fifty thousand miles away since jumping in and out of Havana is not kosher. So I prayed for this important friend and hoped he had not suffered in his dying. I owe so much to Don's support, truthfully my career!

Massimo arrived for a weekend with the money they needed, and by now we were somewhere around one month since my arrival. I asked Massimo to meet with Demitri to begin orchestrating the songs Massimo had composed. Abel was in the show, but I also asked him to work with Demitri on his songs. But, as in Cuban fashion, when Massimo went to Demetri's house, Demetri was not home. When Massimo went back, Demetri was having trouble getting the music software to work. So Massimo went to the beach. Oh, those Italians!

I was the subject of four main press conferences, each with fifteen or more Cuban newspapers and radio stations. I was very impressed with their interest in the show. Laura was a gem at these events and gave me the freedom to just open up. The press wondered how I knew about things like the Pedro Pan exodus and could use it so effectively in the show. They were especially attentive to what I told them was the main point, theme, of my script, which I stated was "Personal freedom, without which, no country can succeed." After a number of these press conferences, as well as an appearance on Cuban television, where I expressed my belief in freedom, I began to realize why Zacchuur said I would perform something of great value for the Cuban people and for Cuba. My mentioning freedom at press conferences caused those authors to write the word freedom as the central theme of their articles.

When I first arrived in Havana, I did again what I had done two years earlier. I went to the US Interests Section and told them where I was staying. This time our "ambassador" (i.e., chief of missions), Michael Parmly, invited me for drinks to "our" residence in Cuba. The day I was to go there, I came home early, took a shower, and dressed in a clean dry shirt, slacks, and threw over my shoulder a sweater for the cool night return. Our American resident property is in Cubanacan, a distance out of Havana. Cubanacan is a limited area where those Americans working at the Interests Section are permitted to live. Otherwise they are not permitted to travel the country.

I hailed a cab on Calle Infanta in the slums of Centro Havana. The driver was very old and frail. His nephew sat next to him. The driver spoke no English, the nephew little. They gave me a price, one way, eleven dollars, which meant it was quite a distance from Calle Infanta. So we began the journey out of Havana, through Miramar, passed Santa Fe, and into Cubanacan. Once there the driver could not find the address. I had shown him the address from the piece of paper Parmly's office had given me so I knew he understood what the correct address was.

We spent forty minutes going up and down Cubanacan, and they checked the little piece of paper about six times. Finally, they turned and asked, "*Eso hombre importante hombre?*"

"*Si.*"

"*Viva en grande casa?*"

I shrugged my shoulder that it was possible. Then they made two turns and pulled up to high hedges and wrought iron gates where Marines guarded the estate. As the cab pulled close to the closed gates, a Marine came to the cab and spoke.

"Tony Giordano?"

"Yes."

My driver and his nephew had "Who the hell is this guy that we picked up in the slums?" look on their faces! I suspect those two men are still laughing.

I paid them and they drove away. Then the Marine sent me up to the great wonderful granite mansion Franklin Roosevelt wintered in and we now have as our "ambassador's" residence built with that Cuban granite I love so much. Plus our property had really green grass, and everything else, a pool, tennis courts, our own water generator. Gorgeous. I like calling it our property in fantasy, but in reality, I felt it was mine. After all, what other American ever worked, legally, in Cuba in two trips for a total of four months since 1960.

I was ushered in by an elderly Cuban housekeeper and brought to Michael Parmly. They offered me a drink and I requested a mojito, which made by this Cuban woman was magnificent. Michael's mother, Marie, was visiting for two weeks so she joined us. Both Michael and his mother are class acts. His wife had not arrived from a recent trip home to France.

Occasionally when I almost began to say something one might have found too bold for Cuba, or even mentioning "Fidel Castro made a mess of the infrastructure of Cuba," Michael would instantly put his finger to his nose and point from there to the ceiling, indicating microphones and people listening. I got the message, and in time Michael suggested that the three of us take a walk and see the grounds. From the area at the pool he spoke of the fact that this house is bugged and we are in Cuba under tough scrutiny. When Michael found out that I was provided a visa for three months and I showed it to him, he was shocked. His mother was only permitted two weeks. "They must really love you, Tony," was Michael's response. When my visit was completed Michael gave me a brochure of the estate, which thrilled Melba and Monica when I returned to Centro Havana.

Throughout the second month Demitri continued to find excuses to avoid rehearsals. Hopefully he knew how to orchestrate, but he did not know how to act as the musical director, not my first time confronting this problem. Massimo returned another time with more money. Rolands, the choreographer, was working as hard as I was, and the designer was creating terrific sets and costumes. I had told him that I loved the architecture of the Malecón, and because my script took place with the Malecón as a backdrop, I asked him to design cloth panels with those great, though destroyed buildings that face the ocean. The panels could be lifted to reveal the sets necessary for all other scenes.

I loved my slow walk to rehearsals in the mornings with my deadened legs as I watched Cubans going to and from their jobs. I had to pass the government's headquarters, and there was always a policeman outside with a large pad for taking notes. The government knew my activities. They had provided me a three-month visa and work permit, so whenever I had to show papers, I was well treated. For instance, each time I went to the US Interests Section, it required that I first speak to the Cuban police on one side of the street. He would okay my walk across the street to the Cuban soldier with guns on the other side of the street. The Cuban soldier would allow me to speak with the Cuban in a wooden booth. The Cuban in the booth would check my papers and approve my walk to a gate in the middle of the block with Marines inside the gates. The Marines would open the gate for me to enter, then make me empty my pockets and walk through the x-ray machines until I was then permitted entrance into the Swedish building that we borrow for our Interests Section. I was starring in a spy thriller.

This US Interests Section is at the Malecón facing Cuba's museum of flags, fifty extremely tall poles with their colorful flags flapping against the ocean. When you stand beneath these flags and look up, they become a ballet company of beautiful women whose skirts rise with the wind for that perfect view. The second time I was in Cuba, the Cubans had changed these to black flags as a protest against George Bush for tightening the embargo, but for me the beauty remained. I'm not certain the Cubans are capable of creating something ugly. Politics did that for them.

I looked forward to rehearsals because my cast was so warm and gracious and always easy to deal with. Cubans never pass you without some affectionate gesture, usually a hug and a kiss, a *"Buena dias"* or *"Buenos noches."* The cast was now acting and with believability. But the choreographer, Isidro Rolands, began to show me several dance numbers, and I was very disappointed. They were well done, but they were terribly old-fashioned. I had not realized how backward their style would be, but I began to understand that I now had the movements from La Tropicana in the days of Batista. I held another production meeting to attempt to improve the choreography and explain that I had hoped for more modern dance, but this only caused Isidro to come to me weeping the next morning, saying he knew I wasn't pleased with him. "I have done badly for you." So now I had to prove to him that his work was excellent. He made numerous adjustments but never shook La Tropicana from the show. The real problem was these rehearsals presented absolutely no method by which I could alter the script. The Spanish language was not mine. I had no computer and my little lamp had no desk. At night I was freezing my swollen knee. It amused me that I was in this situation. After all, from any professional standard this rehearsal period was absurd. Worse, I had no give and take from my collaborators. We couldn't talk to each other about style, story, character or dialogue. So I did what life has taught me: grin and bear it. Then pray.

I am not complaining, since this entire trip was a weird Alice in Wonderland. And while I do agree, "There's no place like home," I was not unhappy. Besides, I never intended for this to be a fully realized production. It was only the press who kept asking if I was bringing the show to Broadway. Cubans all want the ultimate without taking the means to the ends. I answered the Broadway question in a Cuban TV interview by saying it was unlikely since both countries have resistance to the visas that would be necessary. After the show, Castro's government called Compañía Danza de Nacional Contemporánea and told them they were upset with my answer. It was to them strictly America's fault, which was really odd since Cubans are forced to die on balsas from trying to escape the island, while those whose foot touches American soil we embrace immediately as citizens.

Getting ready for that TV interview was interesting. The cameraman and the Cuban woman who would interview me were speaking and gesturing in an odd way. I asked Laura, "What's going on?"

"He is telling her that he will not shoot your face. He will keep the camera just below you chin."

"Why?"

"So no one in America will know you are here."

"Tell them George Bush knows I'm here."

So Laura did. They tried to deal with this, but surprise was painted all over their faces.

I had just sent a letter to President Bush through Michael Parmley's office pouch, telling President Bush I was in Havana and hoped he would help me bring the show to the States if I could find money to tour our schools. I had total trust that, if President Bush received my note, he would try to help. Without realizing the danger I had typed my letter to our President on Carlos Torrens' computer. For the next week Carlos was in panic that Fidel's regime would take away his computer. Because I was welcomed in our Interests Section, visited with our Chief of Missions for drinks, and "friends" with George W. Bush I was becoming suspect as a spy or a CIA operative. What fun!

During the third month of rehearsals, I demanded that someone be hired who could at least play the piano so we could start to sing any songs that were finally orchestrated, because Demitri continued to complain there was too much for him to orchestrate, and his equipment was inadequate, so he was unable to come to rehearsals. Then I began to see clearly that Gretel really couldn't sing. The pianist couldn't play the piano either. But Gretel had no range. She was a wonderful Maryanne, but she had to sing love songs with our Miguel, Carmelo, who had a great Cuban voice. The contrast was horrifying. Imagine a concert between John Denver and Ida Lupino.

During this time, the managers suggested I recast Gretel, so I asked Demitri whether she would be able to come through. He told me she would get through this, though now that I think about it, I'm not certain he ever heard her even try to sing. Plus I felt we all knew her limitations. Why insult her by taking her away from the show? Ironically, the better our production became the thirstier my collaborators became to take the show to New York. To them, I was creating a good production while to me it was simply an inadequate workshop.

Due to the late orchestrations, I cut Maryanne's father's one big song, a five part opera from the show, to lighten the load on Demitri, who was obviously in over his head. So now Pedro was this huge stiffness on stage without even the song I cast him for. Pedro came to me, weeping.

"*Maestro, ninguna cancion para Pedro?*"

"Oh my God, you're right, you have no song. Laura, tell him I'll write him one tonight."

Pedro relaxed as if his problem was resolved. I wondered what the hell I was talking about. I travel through Havana without any fear of trouble, and for some reason I never have any. In Cuba I am indomitable. So I wrote "The Pedro Pan" song and brought it with me the next day, and the first five who read it after Carlos translated it immediately loved it. I figured they were placating me, but that song wound up in the show and created commotion when I taped the performance. Afterward members of ABC, AP, NBC, Cuban television, the Castro government, and our staff from the United States Interestes Section who came to the first performance, pulled me aside.

"You got this script authorized from the Castro government with that song?"

The answer was yes, but the authorization occurred prior to my writing the Pedro Pan song. Together with a later scene where Abel and friends sing as they build a balsa and escape Cuba, the entire show had taken on an unintended condemnation of Cuba, especially since my Pedro Pan song and the scene leading into it express Charles's disdain for Cuba. He sings that he escaped this island as a child and never intended to return, but because of Maryanne's stubbornness he is being forced to return to his nightmare. On my website go to *Habana Carnaval* and press the pictures, which will become videos. (www.tonygiordano.us)

My only concern was to give Pedro a song. And, naturally, by this point in developing my show, I no longer had any awareness of the need to placate the regime in Cuba. In its place I was simply telling the truth as if I was still in the United States, with our oh-say-can-you-see God bless American freedom.

Demitri arrived with his orchestrations during the final week of rehearsal, and as I watched with his musicians, I argued that they would drown out any possibility of ever hearing anyone singing even if they could sing. Demitri wondered why I didn't fire Gretel, forgetting his support of her only several weeks earlier and accepting no responsibility for having failed to help her. In fact, except for Laura, Monica, Melba, and my cast, most of the "adults" I met in Cuba lack maturity. Without the right to vote, to own property, to speak openly, plus having grown up and being told "Leave us alone and go out and play, don't bother us," they are undeveloped. They don't have the courage to fix what they are failing at. To me, this is the saddest of all things about Cuba.

The other saddest thing is that because I was an American, I had no right to any medical care for my legs and my broken knee. Monica, my landlady/doctor said she would sneak me into the hospital if she could find an orthopedic doctor willing to help me, in secret, but she never could. So when Michael Moore films a Cuban hospital, then tells Americans that Cubans have what we need, I say shoot Michael Moore, for he is a liar. Then send him to Cuba with broken legs, without his cameras and without his jet plane; and don't let him use Sean Penn's plane either.

During the last few weeks, my cast became friendly enough to tell me how hungry they were. They exercised as part of the company every morning and came to rehearsals with me every afternoon. There was a dirty kitchen that cooked something for them daily, but apparently it was insufficient. As weird as this is to tell you, one day I took the hard-boiled egg I'd brought with me and gave it to three of my male dancers to divide, right after they finished eating the meal provided for them, telling them I would bring more eggs the next day. When I spoke to Massimo, now that he was calling me once a week, and told him about the cast's hunger, he told me he had included money for their food. Little by little I was discovering just how much Massimo and his friends were paying, and it turned out that all the money they raised to tour the show was now being given to the Cubans in charge of this production who divided the money into serious fees for themselves outside the eyes of the Castro regime, a sport typical in Cuba. I went to the managers and demanded the dancers receive better food, openly letting them know I now knew. Within a day everything changed.

"Tony, come into the kitchen and get something to eat."

"Tony, we brought in boxes of sandwiches. Come and get some."

I tried to tell Massimo to stop with the money already, but Massimo has the kind of good heart and desire for success that says, "If this is what it takes, fuck it, take the money," in his very Italian way. By the time we opened the show and left Cuba, he had given these men every cent he'd raised. So we had not one peso to tour. Massimo has no confrontation skills. Welcome to life in the twenty-first century!

Finally, we could go into Teatro Nacional for tech and hope the show can come together at least so the taping would record something. Teatro Nacional is Cuba's largest theatre, which was right next to our rehearsal studios. We could tech for three and a half days. Massimo hired a Cuban to tape a performance to bring something back to America. I chose the first performance, thinking we might as well, especially because in Cuba the regime cancels things if and when Fidel wants to speak, march, bitch, or complain; and the week we were to give four performances Castro, Morales, and Chavez were five hundred yards away at the *Plaza de la Revolución,* having their May Day rally, threatening to cancel our performances to keep traffic clear.

So, Monday morning we all met in front of Teatro Nacional and waited in the heat. And waited. And waited. Why, you ask? Because no one knew where the key was. Who was the commissioner of the key became an entire day's question and was never solved. Someone in Cuba had the key, and no one knew who he was. So, first tech day spent outside the building.

Tuesday, they discovered who the commissioner was and arrived with the key. So we entered this cavernous space. As with the locked theatre, someone had the key for the lights and the light board, but who? So calls were made to figure this out, and obviously we could not rehearse in the dark. Trust me, I tried.

Several hours later the commissioner of the key for the lights was found and by the end of the second day the lights were lit. The space was enormous, but I never say die. But no one knew how to lower the orchestra pit. Honestly! And the orchestra pit was about sixty-five feet wide. This time I figured why not try to bring the show forward, and put the orchestra upstage behind the actors. But the long drapes with the Malecón architecture painted upon them would have no pipes to hang from. Plus, attempts I made to try this idea upon one or two songs drowned out the singers. So, second tech day, destroyed.

Early the third morning, Laura and I sat alone on an empty stage in semi-darkness as if we were waiting for Godot when two guys looking like thugs arrived from deep away in the opposite direction, carrying a sizeable weapon. Laura didn't know who they were. I asked her what they were carrying. She went over to ask. A crowbar was the answer. Then these two guys began to pry open the orchestra pit inch-by-inch all around the huge oval pit as if it was a can of tuna fish. When they finished, one of them went into the wings, pressed a button, and the entire orchestra pit slowly lowered. This was the afternoon of my third tech day. We now had half a day left, an empty stage, the key to enter the theatre and the key to turn on the lights. Wow! Took only three days. Then we had an audience tomorrow night with the taping. Fortunately I began to envision the day I would be remembering this, which amused me, and at this moment, while writing, I am amused. In Latin there is an expression, *Forsan, et haec olim meminiesse juvabit.* The short version is simple: Have no regrets. The long version is more satisfying but has only an explanation: whenever we suffer some pain, and recall it at a later time, we can only recall it in joy, because the pain is over.

But the worst was yet to come. Now we could tech, except there was no microphone system. I had a Madison Garden space, an overly orchestrated set of brass and bongos, a cast who could not sing, no personal microphones, no microphone system and an audience scheduled with a video taping. A call was made for a microphones specialist, which in Cuba has no meaning because specialists are simply people who can turn on a light or plug in a microphone. Fortunately, the specialists lived only one hour away, so they guaranteed it would only take him two hours to get to us. When he arrived three hours later, he began hanging microphones suspended on thirty-foot cords from the grid, directly over the heads of the cast, which meant I had to push all of the blocking upstage to be under the microphones. Laura kept checking to see when my blood would pour through my skull while I remained in shock. I had been spoiled throughout my career with great designers and technicians, the best virtue within our American theatre. Now I was paying for the good years. Ananke, you bitch!

Finally we were about to start the morning of the fourth day when one manager came to me and asked what I wanted him to do.

"About what?" I foolishly asked, translated through Laura.

"Stage-managing the show."

"But you never saw a rehearsal."

"I know, so tell me what you want."

What I should have told him I wanted, if I spoke the language, was to kill me.

"Where's your head set?"

"We don't have any."

"Anywhere?"

"Right. We don't have head sets."

"How will you be able to call the show?"

"Call the show?"

"Tell lights up behind the top balcony eight thousand feet from here, the conductor out of your view in that dungeon below, and the man hidden on the other side of the stage who is planning to move sets on and off, when to begin or end a scene or a song."

To which this "stage manager?" said, "They'll have to take their own cues."

Since I had discovered no doctor in Cuba would check out my knee, I was certain none would care if I went brain dead. Remain calm was my note to myself. I began to tell him what cues he had to call while he wrote what I was telling him on a piece of paper in the palm of his hand, during which time I suppressed my fury until I lost all sanity and began to laugh uncontrollably.

I never had a daughter, but none could have ever been better for me than Laura, and no proof of that was more obvious than this next moment. She told this man, who was her uncle it turns out, to come back later. She sat me down in the first row like a daughter who is discovering that her father is about to go crazy. She obviously realized that I had lost it. All my verve and bluster evaporated, blood left my face. Suddenly I was panicking and Laura became a woman to rescue this dying director. She asked me to explain stage-managing. I knew the greatness of this girl so I knew she could do what I told her.

I told her the stage manager needs to be able to prepare for the call by checking first that everything about to go into operation is properly prepared by giving a warning of what is about to happen to each of the stage elements, props, sets, lights, music, actors, furniture and then, on "Go," give the cue so all the elements work simultaneously.

When I finished, Laura stood up, climbed onto the stage, and I didn't see her again until after the taping later that night except in and out of the stage wings as she managed to save whatever we might call this show. Laura, being magical and wanting me to succeed abandoned her role as my translator and went to her uncle's side and made the show happen.

I weep as I write with the awareness of what greatness can be. This girl had never left the corner she was born on. She was the dream come true in all of our lives. I stay in touch with her now through email. She is working in Spain. I pray for her, and delight in every good thing that happens to her. For while I constantly bitch about the mess our world is in, I must confess that I have often met the Lauras of this world. I am a spoiled brat who wants everyone to be Laura.

And certainly many more people can be as good. We must reach out and give those in need a chance. My nephew Michael Patella now lives with me, is going to college, and is as great a guy as I had known he could be. Zak Kostro, who graduated from Columbia maxima cum laude in Spanish Lit, is off fighting the good fight in Hollywood towards his acting future. My godson, Johnny Snow, and his brother, Daniel will lead us in everything they do. These educated young people are our future and since my generation failed America it is urgent we pray that those who follow us succeed.

The thirty microphones hanging from the rafters were useless, even after I told the cast to abandon blocking and find a mic to sing into. Can you appreciate a life in the theatre as a well-reviewed director having to resort to the lowest methods of putting on a show? Oh well, I guess at least that made me professional enough to do whatever was necessary rather than walk away. Finally I realized we had two handheld microphones. So I told the cast to pass them around as often as they could, openly, without trying to hide them from the audience. The rest you can see on my website: www.tonygiordano.us. Find scenes, then pictures, click and they will become videos. I had to tape the show, even at its worst, and even I will confess it improved vastly over the weekend, but who knew we would have a weekend?

The very last thing I learned at Teatro Nacional was from a conversation I tried to have with Demetri across our language barriers on my last night there, without Laura to translate. I explained my disappointment that Massimo's songs were too late in being orchestrated and as a result they were not able to help move the second act to its emotional conclusion. Demetri revealed that Cubans don't want to confront those emotions. The first act, which has salsa, mambo rhythms, etc. was easy for them to perform because it was an expression of fun, and basically, of avoidance, but to sing out the frustrations, the lost hopes, the fears for their futures, absolutely not. Cubans live with that outer expression abused people develop for protection: "I'm so happy. Nothing is wrong."

Before we left Cuba together, Massimo gave the managers what he called "The rest of the money." I brought back Cohiba Esplendidos cigars at $500 a box, only to be told that was cheap. In London they sell for $1100 a box. I've never tasted one, but friends love them. And, as I have experienced throughout my career, that first view of Manhattan took my breath away.

When I reflect on the irony that I might have done some good for Cuba in Zucchuur's prophecy, it amuses me that I had to do it in the style of chaotic farce. I would have picked an Ibsen drama. But the farce is more truthful. Somehow in my work I have always had fun, and been silly, and the same holds true in my life. People who have the silliest quirks interest me because I simply love the basics in life. I never seek escape from God's creation. Our lives, our daily struggles, our joy, our hopes are sufficient to me, so my experience in Cuba was perfect because there was no escape from brute reality. Only when I confront moral corruption do I go bonkers. I seem to have an insatiable desire to protect the little guy, while simultaneously wanting to kick his ass for being the little guy. There are days since Cuba when I suspect that the best future for me would be continual journeys, from one corner of the earth to the other, directing plays in languages I cannot speak, read, or understand. Say, for instance, *Hamlet* in North Koreo, *The Eumenides* in Beijing, *The Cherry Orchard* in Pakistan, and on and on. I love this earth. Cuba taught me to realize how much I love to create, even under the worst circumstances.

✻

WE ALL KNOW THAT CUBA has maintained beautiful cars from the forties. And this is true. I stood on the terrace from our fourth floor apartment early mornings as I drank coffee and in the evenings before and after dinner. During those times I would occasionally see one of these fantastic museum cars. I must tell you they are astonishing because the Cubans found ways to maintain them. They look new, and I mean new. They have absolutely no marks, scratches, or dents. But also, they still have colors the rest of the world has abandoned. Red, blue, green, yellow, white in a gloss against the original chromes leap out above the darken aged streets with a level of beauty, only comparable to opening a coffin and finding the incorrupt head of Helen of Troy. How the Cubans have found the paints to match the original colors or the mechanical talents to sustain the beauty of these cars is a mystery to everyone. I came to the realization that Cuba should create a car and manufacture it for the world. This, even more than their cigars, could be the answer to their economy. But, of course, forty-eight years of submission destroys entrepreneurship. Cuban capitalists evaporated and escaped to Miami in an early morning fog as Fidel's cabin cruiser, *Granma,* was docking in 1959. Thereafter the grandeur of this island decayed, but the people survived. They in fact maintain at least as much humanity as I see among people in America, perhaps no more, but I guarantee, no less.

✻

MY EXPERIENCES IN CUBA are further defined. At the beginning of my last week in Cuba Massimo called and asked if I could find a way to allow his Cuban girlfriend's four friends to attain their visas from the Interests Section to the U.S. Apparently they were unable to get into the building. So two hours prior to my second day of tech I walked in the opposite direction, arrived, and proceeded to go through all the grinding steps it required for me to get in. Afterwards I walked several miles to my tech rehearsal. That night Massimo called to ask if I had found the time and I told him I did. He asked what he needed to tell the Cubans about how they could get into the building to get visas. I told him there was no need for them to go there. He was disappointed that they could not get their visas, until I revealed that he needed to tell them to come to me.

"Why you?"

"Because I have the four visas."

"You have their visas?'

"Yes."

"They gave you the visas of people you don't even know?"

"Yes."

My life in Cuba caused me to be suspect among the Cubans I stayed with, who witnessed things like this and truly believed I worked for the CIA.

When I was back from Cuba for one month, I received a letter from our State Department, telling me President George W. Bush asked them to aid me in lifting visas for Cuban dancers. They said in their letter that it took them a little time to write to me because they had searched their files and they could not locate any early paperwork where I had asked them first, was turned down, and then went to the President. But, frankly, I love President George W. Bush and believe he has been maligned for so many diverse reasons. So when I asked Michael Parmly to send it to the White House in a pouch out of Havana I trusted that George W. Bush would help, as my mother had trusted in me on her deathbed, "I don't even have to ask. I know you will always keep an eye out for your sister." She knew I would. I knew I would. Real people have no reason to hide. Only EENY, MEENY, MINY or MO do that. So I went to D.C. and met with the State Department, but alas we had no money to proceed with the project. Massimo paid my collaborators every last cent.

※

DURING THE FOUR MONTHS I lived in Cuba it was clear to me that socialism/communism was no help to Cuba. And clearly Fidel Castro and his ideology hated capitalism more than their disbelief in God Himself so the ism in Capitalism would not help either. What did that leave? In my opinion, Humanism! The many hot afternoons I dragged two dead legs across the broken structures of Havana, saw dogs collapse against the scolding pavements, and smelled coals ignited atop grills inside someone's home, without of course air vents, allowing the smoke to engulf their living space. Somehow Cuban la gente survives with or without toilet seats and other amenities.

La gente, the world over, are Americans, Europeans, Africans, Indians, Asians and Cubans who share the art of men acting. They laugh, love, hate and cry as we do. Cubans are clean. They use old rags to clean their walls, their floors and hallways, then wash and dry that rag for another day's service. Their children are scrubbed and ironed, each morning, and sent off to school. Cubans are people, so despite the ism they live under they behave in the same manner as my parents did, here in U.S.A. People prove their worth whenever they are forced to do so, and that is how man continues to survive. The error people make, however, is in not recognizing their greatness so they assume they need leaders to do for them what, supposedly, they cannot do for themselves. Then they learn to obey the evils of their leaders and pay taxes accordingly.

And Cuba is a magnificent island. In the full geography of its circumference, its magical fresh air, its variety of terrains, its cluster of towns, its vegetation, birds and fish it might in fact become the perfect chance for us to try something new to live well on planet Earth. Why should any ism be necessary? Why does any ism, anywhere, in every country, ours as well, always seem to defeat the lives of the people? How can any ism be sufficient in itself? Capitalism has its flaws, its good points. Socialism is intended to be camaraderie. Communism demands total commitment to the state. They all have their salient points though none of the isms work anywhere and certainly not in Cuba. But what if we took from column A and column B and blended? We do not do this because the Castro's, Obama's, Putin's refuse to accept blends. Their inflexibility is unable to fulfill its ideology so they justify catastrophe for the people as proof of their ongoing support for their stupid ideology.

Fidel conquered a great island and I would like to believe he thought his plan was the right one. But without the entrepreneurial participation from the la gente who fled, Fidel failed. I realize that such failure may be seen by Castro to be success, but I am speaking for myself. A society fails when it lacks individuality, freedom, open discourse, personal ownership, and collaboration in leadership, not to mention dilapidated streets and houses, once gorgeous colonial architecture. Even though Commissioner Eubesio Leah is beautifully restoring some buildings it is not enough to matter, especially in such sharp contrast with the shattered homes that exist everywhere.

It became clear to me that the isms of our world intrude upon the greatness intended for our lives, partially because too many of the leaders who forge their particular ism are inadequate to the task, and often too corrupt, and intolerant of including within their ism its opposing ism. Sorry for the difficult turn of phrases. I am trying to say *why the fuck do we need so much government?* Why do we the people not control our fates? Why do we permit those in charge to take away our ability to kick their ass and throw them out of office when they betray their service to us, their misuse of our money, their insistence that they have our answers? Why do we not face each other and have it out, in the public square, the parent/faculty school nights, the government buildings?

I find one sidedness impossible to deal with. And in my lifetime one sidedness is all I see. Pundits argue passionately for their cause, their candidate, their use of a society's income to win, but they refuse to acknowledge that their cause, candidate, and our income require more than one method to properly service any society. Cuba could become a shining example, a model throughout the world to demonstrate the art of men acting especially with the proof today that Cuba has failed and is anxiously wondering how to proceed. Just waiting for Fidel and Raul to die does not a solution make. Cuba, and the rest of our world need new approaches.

For America is also failing. The big elephant called America Fidel wants to defeat is failing at the same pace as his tiny mouse. Both countries need not health care but health cure. What if both countries need the same cure? I went to Cuba believing we have too much, and they have too little and that part of my assumption was absolutely correct. What I discovered was that we had something in common. In both countries individual freedoms do not exist, though our country brags about our wonderful freedoms. Cuba has no freedom, America has freedom in name only.

Entrepreneurial Cubans live in Florida, New York, Los Angeles, Chicago, Philadelphia and all points in between and have been extremely successful in America. But their businesses, and worse, their beautiful homes throughout Cuba are demolished, while the Cubans who joined the regimes, as well as other Cubans who simply remained have no tools, no guns, no finances, no power to fix their decaying country. Cuba's la gente need the Cuban Americans and Cuban Americans need the Cuban la gente, if for no other reason than to make being a Cuban whole again. They suffered a tragic division and there is no reason to create longstanding hostility when they could view each other as a diaspora.

However, the Cuban community in America resents the Cuban community in Cuba. And vice versa. There is no love lost between these two forces. I know this is a strange opinion, especially in view of the amount of money American Cubans send each year to their relatives in Cuba to help them survive or build a balsa to brave shark filled waters. And frankly this is one particular I hope I am wrong about. No one told this to me. I came to my own opinion. It is possible I am one of very few Americans who have worked, legally, in Cuba for the past sixty years. However, admittedly, I do not speak the language, so take my opinions with a grain of salt.

I made a serious attempt to bring both sides together, ambos mundo, when I returned to the United States and that's when I found myself looking at this issue with 20/20 vision. It was clear within the first ten phone calls that such a combination of efforts, here and there, would never work. *Choose us, or them. They stayed with him and lived in our homes, which we want back. They believed in Castro. We knew better. We survived, thanks to America but mostly thanks to the fact that we are the entrepreneurs Cuba needed all along. Those who stayed behind succumbed to Fidel's ism, lived and destroyed our property and proved to be undesirable to us. We cannot work with them.*

And ever it is thus. Warring families. Warring societies, countries, friends, schools of thought, the curse goes on and on. In great literature there are at least two great examples of what drama can do to help us through this dynamic within the art of men acting. I suspect that my odyssey brought me to Canada, to direct *Long Day's Journey Into Night* so I could meditate upon its uncanny resemblance to America's troubles; brought me to Brussels so I could delve into the fears created by every ethnic group when they immigrate into societies that hate them; brought me to Cuba so I could view the degradation of socialism. In each of these journeys I was able to witness the drama of life, equal or better than the drama of theatre, but in each case it made me realize how theatre can be of value to resolve these matters.

Aeschylus took warring enmity between opposing groups as a dramatic topic and wrote a trilogy, called *The Oresteia* with its three plays: *Agamemnon, The Choephori, and The Eumenides*. According to encyclopedias *The Oresteia* uses the legend of the family of Atreus as raw material for examination of different aspects of such questions as the nature of justice, methods of establishing and maintaining justice on earth, the relationship of justice to vengeance, mercy, the gods, fate, and the social order. It also deals with the related doctrines that wisdom can be learned only through experience and suffering, that one crime invariably leads to another if the criminal is not punished, that blood, once shed, can never be atoned for, and that authority is the foundation of civilization.

In the second play the FURIES pursue Orestes to avenge the murder he committed.

But due to the convolution of the family history of events that led to the necessity, if you will, of this murder the FURIES are turned into the third play, EUMENIDIES, that is, into softer, sweeter justices and forgive Orestes rather than kill him, and are then provided a seat at the table of Athenian legislation. Compromise and understanding came together and all is well.

Shakespeare creates PORTIA, the most highly evolved character in all of dramatic literature and she manages to find the same means of justice and mercy to resolve a similar ongoing revenge in *The Merchant of Venice*.

Drama guides us. Where is a play today to help us view ourselves and/or cure any one of our curses? Sticking at this time just to Cuba, let me suggest that Castro probably began with the best intentions. Even I found in Cuba the terrain and footprint of the gem of the ocean. I can easily surmise how Fidel told himself he was not about to let the progress of the world encroach upon his treasure. So he decided to prevent all intrusions. But, as I've personally discovered one person's idea is not sufficient to bring success if it is inflexible, limited to the mind of just that one person.

God is the perfect example of how this should work. He created all things and gave to Humanity free will, the ability to tell God off, if and whenever you choose to do so. Yet he provided all the gifts of life we need while we are toying with our free will to discover Him and willingly go back to Him.

My point is that ever since I spent time in Cuba I tapped into my hope that the Cubans resolve their societal problems. What I discovered was how productive America Cubans are and while I was in Cuba I discovered how nice Cuban la gente are. Together, it seems to me, is the perfect balance for a special culture. They should become one and put their best feet forward towards their triumph over the past fifty years, and they must create new ways that work for both sides of this coin.

I believe they should even embrace Fidel's plan but coupled with the capitalism Cubans perfect so well in America. It is just possible that Cuba could become a microcosm of Utopian Humanity for the rest of the world to witness. Just send ten thousand artisans with one hundred billion dollars and restore this great island. Perhaps it could become a splendid cultural center for the world. If my career ever winds up in film I would love to create a movie to dramatize an attempt to create such a cultural country. I would choose Cuba as the example. But whether I am lucky enough for such a dream I must confess I have never truly left Cuba. My heart often is stuck, in love with the last project I directed, but with Cuba I find myself sorry I left. I miss the sense of something I cannot define, perhaps a sense that I wish I could have fulfilled the work even better than I did, though I admit it was way ahead of any plan I had to begin with.

Capitalism will not defeat us. Nor socialism. Or communism.

What will defeat us is lack of humanity.

CHAPTER EIGHTEEN

MO'S are people you brush shoulders with daily.

At Manhattan Plaza, those who secretly whisper that the Plaza is corrupt but refuse to be interviewed, or when they are interviewed refuse to admit what they know for fear of reprisal, are Mo's. Ask them about their "Proud Tenant's President", they'll tell you she's in the pocket of management, but don't wait for them to do anything to stop that. Other tenants hide their true incomes, so once again taxpayers are being screwed from both ends of this entitlement program.

Mo's are everywhere.

For instance, when I went back to Maine to direct *The Lion in Winter*, I allowed my better judgment to be compromised. The Portland theatre suggested an actress for Eleanor of Aquitaine, and I agreed to audition her. I discovered she had played the role previously. I prefer actors who have never played the role. I will now call this actress, Lady Mo. I accepted her guarantee that she was a professional who would in no way make me sorry, that she would rehearse ready, willing and able to create as if from her tabula rasa.

But on our first day off at the end of one week of rehearsal, she and I were walking to the parking lot when I asked her how she was feeling about rehearsals. She told me she was very upset that I was directing her by following directions from the actor who was playing Henry. Shocked, I couldn't even understand how she could think such a thing. She then told me that after every time Henry came close to me and we spoke in private, I turned to her and gave her a note that Henry had just told me to give her. Well, at least now I could relate to why she was feeling the way she was, so I explained that "Henry" had been nervous about playing his role. I'd told him at his audition that I was concerned about a certain way he delivers his lines, and he hoped we could work together to fix that. Each time he came close to me and whispered it was to find out if his problem was getting better. He was by nature one of those actors who want support and only interested in that. I tried to explain this to her for two hours, but she would have none of it. So I asked her to take a drive with me so we could resolve this before we re-entered rehearsals the next day. We went to a park and spoke for four more hours, during which time she informed me that she didn't trust me and that I was lying.

Well, years of being known as an actor's director washed down the drain in seconds thanks to this paranoid, Lady Mo. I made every effort to explain that I would never allow an actor to tell me how to direct another actor; that if one actor had anything to say about another actor and I thought it was a decent idea, I would speak about it openly. "Henry thinks you should smack him in the face and I think it's a good idea. What do you think?" so the other actor would be included in the discussion. I explained that even if Henry had ever mentioned her in an aside with me but I had no interest in what his idea might have been I would drop it altogether and proceed instead with whatever my next plan was. I tried to comfort her by saying after Henry speaks to me in rehearsal I usually return to the thought I was about to express prior to his intrusion. In her case, for instance, I had decided to change this actress's entire approach to playing Eleanor. Since I knew she had played it before, and since I did not like her heavy handed approach as she entered the play, I wanted her to start the show more as a queen with a lady inside her, then show her teeth as the play began. So whenever Henry finished his asides to me, I continued to execute my plan.

I cannot understand an actor denying the time I was wasting on my day off to relax her paranoia while she insultingly blamed me and Henry and everything in sight after swearing not to be that kind of actress. Obviously she took no responsibility for her own actions or her promise. By the end of the six hours, I was only able to put a stop to this silliness when finally I revealed what I had wanted never to say: "Henry has never in the course of this week ever mentioned your name, your character, or anything to do with you as an actress or a person, which frankly I find odd considering the role he is playing, and he doesn't even know you have played Eleanor before because to protect you, I've never mentioned it to anyone."

When I went back into rehearsal the next day, I never mentioned my irritating meeting with Lady Mo to anyone. During the second week she claimed she trusted me and said from the way I work and the openness with which I speak in rehearsals that I would never have done what she had thought. I assumed she was sincere and was happy for the turnabout.

As for Henry, he was nervous but moving forward the way an actor at the start of the second week should be moving forward, so I was satisfied with him as well. But she then came and told me he was never going to be a good Henry. Then she began to itemize what I can only assume were comparisons with her other Henry from the previous production. Prior to opening, both of them were good and she told me he was wonderful, but she was now very upset with the actor playing her younger son, who was too confrontational with her. I had clearly directed Seth to be confrontational, openly, in front of her. She must have been comparing him to her previous production's sniveling John, the stereotypical way John is usually played.

The show opened well. I have left out her name to protect the guilty. But at the opening night party, two upsetting things occurred that made it clear she had never stopped her nonsense. First, the managing director came to me during the party and said she was sorry Henry had caused so much trouble for Eleanor. Then Lady Mo came to me before parting. "I want you to know I'm not like that. I don't know what went wrong. I hope we will work together again, so you'll see who I really am." I already know how to spell idiot. I must remember to put a comma after my name first.

What is a Mo since we find them everywhere?

CHAPTER NINETEEN

EDWIN MARKHAM'S "The Man with the Hoe" provides a description that helps me to explain my version of a Mo.

Bowed by the weight of centuries he leans
Upon his hoe and gazes on the ground.
The emptiness of ages in his face.
And on his back the burden of the world.
Who made him dead to rapture and despair,
A thing that grieves not and that never hopes,
Stolid and stunned, a brother to the ox?
Who loosened and let down this brutal jaw?
Whose was the hand that slanted back this brow?
Whose breath blew out the light within this brain?

The Mo's are all those who sleep during their waking hours, who refuse to enter into the world around them, who stand by while everyone else steals, lies, cheats, betrays, destroys. The Mo's do little wrong, because they do little of anything, yet what little they do, they do in evil imitation of the others. Somehow either they assume all is well, or they don't care, or they fear they have no right. In any case, becoming brother to the ox is why the Eenies, Meenies, and Minies manage to get away with all their greed while Mo's function as their willing slaves.

Is this the Thing the Lord God made and gave
To have dominion over sea and land;
To trace the stars and search the heavens for power;
To feel the passion of Eternity?
Is this the dream He dreamed who shaped the suns

And markt their ways upon the ancient deep?
Down all the caverns of Hell to their last gulf
There is no shape more terrible than this—
More tongued with cries against the world's blind greed—
More filled with signs and portents for the soul—
More packt with danger to the universe.

Throughout my personal odyssey, I have loved and hated the average person simultaneously. Yes, I found myself wanting to awake in them the spirit of passion that would cause this world to work. But most of the time these people sit on their hands. So I love them enough to want to imbue them with a greater spirit, but I hate their resistance enough to want to nuke them. I love Markham's poem but differ in that he blames their stolid lives on industrialization. I blame these stolid people themselves. I believe just about everyone has the possibilities to do better, if they want to. And certainly they could do better if they would work together for the common good. Every urge on their part to cheat someone, or beat someone, or overwhelm someone adds up to the crimes that make them slaves to the industrial, military complex.

In my own family, the people I loved were satisfied to be good, warm, nurturing people whose home was a joy to have a meal in, and certainly my father, uncles, brothers, cousins, and their friends went willingly to serve in World War II to fight for our freedom. But once finished, they sat back and let anyone else make this the greedy world it became. They saw greed but assumed because they had none of the greed the greed of others would be corrected by someone else. When they aged, in almost all the cases within my family, they spent their final days in anger and frustration. The world had not managed to give them what they had hoped for, a community of citizens as good as they were. I watched many of them discover the idiocy of our bureaucracy; the denials of our representatives to tell the truth; the criminals who were freed because of clever lawyers. My elders left this world with insatiable grins.

What gulfs between him and the seraphim!
Slave of the wheel of labor, what to him
Are Plato and the swing of Pleiades?

What the long reaches of the peaks of song,
The rift of dawn, the reddening of the rose?
Thru this dread shape the suffering ages look;
Time's tragedy is in that aching stoop;
Thru this dread shape humanity betrayed,
Plundered, profaned and disinherited,
Cries protest to the Powers that made the world,
A protest that is also prophecy.

Flora Roberts, the literary agent who represented Bill Gibson and Vincent Canby, two playwrights whose plays I directed told me she always knew I had a great reputation, but after Vincent Canby and "Especially Bill Gibson, a man not given to making compliments," told her I was a genius (her word, not mine), Flora asked, "So, why are you not more famous?"

"Well, I never cared to be."

"I know," she said. "But everyone talks about how good you are. Why did it not cause you to be more famous?"

I could only tell her the truth as I knew it, because I had not been prepared to have the discussion. "I guess because no one knows the fullness of my work. I went everywhere by myself and left almost all of it behind. I never consolidated."

"Good answer," Flora stated, "Now do something about it."

Then she hung up.

But the real answer is I never cared about fame. Pride in my work, yes, but not fame. I wanted to use my work and its travels to discover God, and I have. I wanted my work to bring me face to face with as many people in life as possible and try to know how to instill in all of us what we need to fill God's world with the success He deserves for having given us life. I found the sadness of a world heading into its own destruction, a destruction of man's creation. I witnessed too many Mos. But I never lost God and that has made all the difference, for I always have hope.

O masters, lords and rulers in all lands,
Is this the handiwork you give to God,

This monstrous thing distorted and soul-quencht?
How will you ever straighten up this shape;
Touch it again with immortality;
Give back the upward looking and the light;
Rebuild in it the music and the dream;
Make right the immemorial infamies,
Perfidious wrongs, immedicable woes?

Education, theatre, the arts, philosophy, poetry, meditation, prayer, charity, social intercourse, debate, confrontation, self evaluation, gardening, the art of reasoning, and active participation in one's own odyssey are tools to make right the immemorial infamies, perfidious wrongs, immedicable woes and lift ourselves into humanity's art of men acting. But those are the ideals, and we live in a world that insists we must accept man's refusal to rise to his higher nature because ever was it thus. Yet, in everything we really want, we know we only achieve it when we embrace the ideal way to achieve it, be it the ability to run a three-minute race better than the next guy, or build a bridge, cook an Italian dinner, play the flute, grow your garden.

My advice is to keep working at goals, especially ideals. Do not be saddened by the many trials and tribulations along the way, even when suddenly out of the human garbage pail another Mo might emerge, as a Mrs. Mo did to me when I was interviewed on her radio show one spring Sunday morning. Within two months, she called and told me she had gone to the local Performing Arts Center and found out that there was no event for Columbus Day. She asked me to join her in creating a show for that date. I told her my background did not include creating that kind of show. She said she had done them. She suggested she would set up a meeting at the center and call me back. We then met with the managing director of the theatre. After learning about some of the terms of renting the theatre I told Mrs. Mo I would give her an answer about collaborating with her if I found a headliner. The next day I called Julius La Rosa, whom I had directed many years ago. He agreed to be the headliner. I then accepted her invitation to become partners in this project.

She told me she was experienced in selling tickets, that she had done this for this theatre previously, and that she could use her radio audience for this purpose, as well as sponsors who could provide financial support. I told her I could write a script, and hire the entertainers to support Julius. I would be in the city for most of this. She would have direct contact with JoAnne Robertozzi, the friend who originally told Mrs Mo to interview me.

I agreed to activate my corporate bank account so we had a legal right to raise money to contract the talent and pay our expenses. I also hired the remaining entertainers and wrote a script for the two-act show. After I hired the entertainers and after Mrs. Mo read the script, which was approximately one month into our collaboration, she told me she was disappointed I did not include her as one of the entertainers. She wanted to be the hostess to introduce each act. I explained that I had not known her plan and, because of the way I'd created the show, it was not possible to satisfy her wishes. I would let her introduce the show to open it, and she could also be the one to bring flowers to the performers from the audience at the end.

Two weeks prior to our show, she called to tell me we had only sold sixty-seven seats (out of 1200). I asked what the prognosis was for a rush at the end. I spoke also to the managing director. It seemed hopeless. Mrs. Mo thought we should cancel. I asked if she would consider joining me in putting up two or three thousand dollars each, so we could still provide a show for the community and the entertainers and take the chance that walk up ticket sales would pay us back. She declined.

I then asked her to split the expenses I had already incurred. Her answer defines most Mo's. "What do you mean? I had nothing to do with this project. I was just helping you." Nothing I told her from that moment on changed her insane lie, except by the time I took her to small claims court, twice, I witnessed her lie under oath. "I was hired by Tony Giordano to be the hostess. I was only helping him out because he rented the theatre to present his musical about Sacco and Vanzetti." She brought a character witness, a young man I'll now call Little Mo, who testified, both times, that Mrs. Mo was telling the truth. Need I mention, Little Mo had never been at any of our meetings or phone calls. I had never met him, yet he perjured himself, twice.

Mrs. Mo and little Mo live with no obligation to truth or conscience.

They choose to be slaves to lying because they believe that is the best way to win a fight to avoid costs. These people are not ensnared within Scylla and Charybdis. They did not challenge life or conquer mythological gods. No. They are ensnared within themselves, caught inside their own skins, stuck to their flaying bones. Imagine what havoc that plays with each of their souls. To lie, under oath, over something so insignificant is a sign of their demise. Lies never escape Ananke. Mrs. Mo and little Mo should have admitted the truth. Instead they chose to suffer outrageous futures by owing Ananke a debt, which has no deadline as to when it needs to be paid. But it will be paid.

> *O masters, lords and rulers in all lands,*
> *How will the future reckon with this Man?*
> *How answer his brute question in that hour*
> *When whirlwinds of rebellion shake all shores?*
> *How will it be with kingdoms and with kings--*
> *With those who shaped him to the thing he is—*
> *When this dumb Terror shall rise to judge the world,*
> *After the silence of the centuries?*
> (Signed: Your Edwin Markham: Staten Island,
Ronald Wyllys Webpage)

CHAPTER TWENTY

I CREATED ANANKE, LTD to produce theatrical products that might alter the downward spiral that is leading us into the end of days. I remind you that Ananke is the goddess of unalterable necessity, fate and destiny, from which one cannot escape. (Plato)

Ananke forces us to fulfill our spiritual life. By completing obligations honorably, paying the costs for truth willingly, and obeying the rules of justice faithfully we save that much of the world we inhabit. Ananke acts out of love. After all, once the boil bursts, puss flows and the body heals. We all die, and while we are here we must obey all the rules of engagement. We, not you, me, him, or her, but "we" need each other to climb through the debris of living. Ananke is brutal in her insistence that we succumb to life, so why not accept her reality?

Ananke forces us, not God, or any religion, to clean our sins. It is as if the soul simply has an automatic clean yourself button. But if we want to cure our selves in advance of Ananke we need honesty. In the event HUD runs out of tax monies and all subsidies become erased, the citizens who bled the taxpayers need to recognize their role in their own demise. Unless, of course, they want to continually blame George Bush. And wouldn't it be tremendous if every problem could always be George Bush's fault? There is no honesty in that. Saddest of all is how people close their eyes to the corruption that surrounds them. And there it is! Good things are vitiated daily by Mo's, the ones who permit the Eeny, Meeny, Miney, and fellow Mo's to corrupt our world.

But show me the playwright willing to disobey political correctness, clichés, or downright lies to expose our suicide. We, in the theatre, have failed the most because we entered the very profession that possesses the greatest obligation to truth. And I in particular failed even more so. I am a true idealist. I pride myself that I face reality, but I was too trusting, hardly reality. I should have done more than cried throughout my life for unknown sufferers. I should have waged war instead of writing letters openly to enemies. I should have gathered an army of idealists and forged a plan, but none of that is within my capabilities. I am a true collaborator. But I am honestly not political. I am the guy who argues openly to the very end.

Edwin Markham wrote "The Man With The Hoe" he says, "To breathe into the lines the spirit of brotherhood, the spirit of social humanity." He wrote it to cry for justice because he felt the man with the hoe is the man "Under the hoofs of the labor world, a slave of drudgery as a victim of industrial oppression." But Mo's are no longer trampled upon through a social inhumanity against them. Unions were established to help workers get benefits and healthy conditions, but these days Mo's have banded together and reached for the powers once held against them. The moment Mo's band together into large groups they turn their power against any individual who doesn't concur with them, proving just how much power Mo's have. Mo's actively participate by not actively fighting against the evils that surround them.

Our society follows leaders who lie to them. Instead of telling the public that happiness depends upon individual responsibility, fools who are desperate for our votes say "Elect me and I will find a way to make all your dreams come true." To me, a leader should be the person who says "I will help the needy and provide the opportunity for the rest of you to help yourselves." I never hear anyone even suggest that poor people might be cheating the system. As long as someone lives in degradation, we always assume someone else did that to them. But, trust me, I have met those who are benefitting from all sources, other than self-reliance, so their journey takes them further and further away from their destiny to succeed.

We must help others to fulfill their odyssey because God's experiment cannot complete itself until all of humanity freely chooses to return to Him. So while it might be fun to think we can compete for God's love, or enjoy revenge thinking of souls we dislike suffering eternal damnation in the fires of hell I do not believe any soul, and I include Hitler in this, can be annihilated. Hitler has to pay for his sins, and then he has to clearly see the evil reality of his ways, sufficient to want God and a total reversal of his crimes and sins. He has to go to God, cleansed, and that journey will be his hell.

I have attempted to demonstrate throughout these three books that family, celebrities, friends, neighbors and strangers share human traits equally. Any part of the body that has cancer affects all other parts of the body. And I say this after a life of failing to change any of the corruptions I confronted. But that is no reason not to keep trying since life is filled with helpful surprises. This morning, Jim Whiting, a classmate from Brooklyn Prep, unaware of what I am writing, sent me this quote that succinctly states what I hope my three books dramatize.

> "A human being should be able to change a diaper, plan an invasion, butcher a hog, conn a ship, design a building, write a sonnet, balance accounts, build a wall, set a bone, comfort the dying, take orders, give orders, cooperate, act alone, solve equations, analyze a new problem, pitch manure, program a computer, cook a tasty meal, fight efficiently, die gallantly. Specialization is for insects."
> Robert Heinlein

※

MYTHS HAVE POWERFUL INFLUENCE upon us and are perhaps much of the cause of our demise, for they overly simplify. I believe, for instance, that we have misinterpreted the Adam and Eve story. I find it hard to accept that eating an apple to acquire some of God's power is sin. I wish Adam had eaten the whole tree. Man needs more of God. Our ultimate dramatic journey is to rise into as much of God as we can achieve. God will always be God and each of us will always be our self, but the closer to God each of us becomes the greater will be the humanity God created as His favorite creation, and the prouder He will be to have us with Him in what I can only assume is a fabulous plan.

So, thank you, Eve. Had you not pushed Adam, we would now be as submissive as Cuba's la gente. Perhaps we can lift ourselves out of our morass through meditation, which might allow God to add higher levels of DNA so we can approach more of His love and greatness. Until we do this and He raises our DNA He certainly has given us a very good excuse to fail Him. We have been God damned. God knew we would use our free will to deny Him, to claim creation as our own, to destroy life and His beautiful planet, so He was stingy on our DNA and knows we will fail. Hopefully we discover that we cannot live without God, his universe, and his spiritual world and either we ask Him for higher DNA or discover that our already existing DNA can be raised into a fourth, fifth, ninth dimension. It certainly would cause the end of our world, as we know it, to rise into greater consciences, love each other, applaud and love God. Wouldn't it be nice to wake up one morning with only the desire to work for our world, not cheat each other and have no need to betray our great life?

✳

I DO NOT BELIEVE IN HELL. This is not perverse on my part. Since I believe everything that exists is God, I find it difficult to assume God could kill parts of Himself. God sent Jesus, His son, to suffer on our behalf, and some might argue then that God killed a part of Himself when Christ, crucified, died. But remember context, Jesus rose three days later, proving there is no death. To me, the New Testament is about the Resurrection. God sent Jesus to suffer terribly and show us resurrection, demonstrating our journey out of this material life into our spiritual life. Ananke will force us to make all the necessary corrections. The completion of our art of men acting ends as one humanity.

We might as well get with the plan because we are doomed to perfection.

APPENDIX

THE FOLLOWING ARE LETTERS to confront corruption at HUD housing and the Department of Labor's creation of the Society of Stage Directors and Choreographers as a national labor union. I chose these as samples because they include full details. This list of names that immediately follows are the recipients of this first letter.

RECIPIENTS OF SAMPLE LETTER # 1

    Honorable Alphonso Jackson (HUD)
    Shaun Donovan (HPD)
    Michael Bloomberg Mayor of New York
    Judith Calagero (Commissioner DHCR)
    Deborah Von Amorongen (HUD , NY)
    Richard Gottried (NY State Assembly)
    Thomas Duane (NY State Senate)
    Manhattan Community Board #4
    Congressman Jerrold Nadler
    Senator Charles Schumer
    Senator Hillary Rodham Clinton
    Alan G Hevesi (NY State Comptroller)
    Elliot Spitzer (NY State Attorney General)
    NY City Councilperson Christine Quinn
    Speaker Gifford Miller (NY City Council)
    Richard Mc Curnin (DHCR)
    Manhattan Borough President C. Virginia Fields
    Bronx Borough President Adolfo Carrion
    Brooklyn Borough President Marty Markowitz
    Staten Island Borough James Molinaro
    Queens Borough Helen Marshall
    Society of Stage Directors and Choreographers
    Screen Actors Guild
    Actors Equity Association
    American Federation of Musicians (Local 802)
    American Federation of Television and Radio Artists
    Tenants and Neighbors
    John Fisher (Westside Coalition)
    Gil Noble (NBC)

Bill O'Reilly (Fox news)
Bill Moyers (PBS)
Tom Robbins (Village Voice)
Ruth Lerner (retired, Commissioner of HPD)
Manhattan Plaza Tenants Association
Manhattan Plaza Policy Making Committee
Stephen Ross, The Related Company
NYC DA Special Prosecutions Bureau

SAMPLE LETTER # 1, addressed to each individual, above. The attached list was included for them to know who else received this letter.

Manhattan Plaza Residents Alliance, LLC
400 West 43trd St., #28M, New York, 10036
www.manhattanplazaresidents.org 212-941-xxxx

June 14, 2004

Dear Ladies and Gentlemen,
(see attached list)
RE: Manhattan Plaza, HUD Project Section 8

It is urgent that you investigate the following matter, to correct its wrong and insure accountability.

We believe that for twenty-six years Aquarius management defrauded taxpayers by allocating 168 apartments at Manhattan Plaza to friends and associates instead of complying with the requirements of the 1977 Board of Estimate Resolution (at least 70% performing artists, up to 15% elderly and up to 15% substandard community residents). Now Related Companies has purchased Manhattan Plaza and intends to continue the process.

We ask each of you as politicians, government agencies (HUD) (HPD) and authorized tenant's organizations to freeze any further negotiations by Related Companies, until the fraud is corrected and appropriate retrospective actions taken. Our organization, Manhattan Plaza Resident Alliance, represents those tenants at Manhattan Plaza who do not want taxpayers cheated in our name nor on our behalf. It is important that the 1977 Board of Estimate Resolution be returned to integrity, which is the best method to protect tenants and taxpayers jointly.

Here are the facts. In March 1977 New York City's Board of Estimate voted in favor of the Resolution, mapping out demands and obligations required to maintain the subsidy. The Resolution clearly established the groups for whom the subsidy was intended. But by June 1977 Laila Long, an assistant commissioner of HPD with the aid of Rodney Kirk, manager of Manhattan Plaza, siphoned off 168 apartments to be given out at the owner's discretion to ineligible persons. Ms Long moved into a two-bedroom apartment.

It appears that Ms Long and Mr. Kirk falsified, in person, to the Policy Committee that the government asked them to do this. The policy committee was unable, at that time, to recognize the fraud, so the 168 apartments were extracted from the Board of Estimate's requirements and treated as a separate list to be used instead for friends, and associates of the owners. Finally, in 1986–87 the policy committee realized the possibility of fraud, and demanded proof. Only an incriminating "memo to files" in Ms Long's office was presented, stating that she and Rodney Kirk decided to re-allocate 168 apartments. ("Memo to the files")

In an effort to correct this fraud the Policy Committee in 1987 voted unanimously (cf. attached 'minutes') that 100% of the apartments were allocated as per the Board of Estimate Resolution (at least 70% performing artists, 15% elderly and 15% substandard community residents). Despite this unanimous decision Aquarius Management refused to release the list and maintained these apartments separately. Now they have sold Manhattan Plaza as if those 168 apartment are legitimately separated from the 100% Section 8.

The significance of all of this is staggering. Those 168 apartments were scheduled for performing artists and funded by the taxpayers. Throughout these years, performing artists were denied apartments because they did not meet strict requirements, while apartments were being allocated to non-performing artists, who met no requirements except friendship with the owners. (cf. Ruth Lerner's letter of 1979) In Ms Lerner's letter you see her concern about lawsuits.

Further, the Board of Estimate Resolution requirement that at least 70% of the building maintain occupancy by performing artists is significant because the misallocated 168 separate apartments were necessary to meet this requirement. Without those 168 apartments there was no possibility that at least 70% could ever be attained.

Also, the Board of Estimate Resolution clearly mandates Manhattan Plaza as a "limited profit housing development." We also understand the mortgage agreement specifically limits the percentage of profit that the owners can make on the apartments. Yet Related Companies is seeking considerable additional yearly profit from taxpayers. How can an obligation to limited profit become an opportunity for unlimited profit?

Let us roughly quantify the tax dollars involved, to put into perspective the tremendous amount of public money that goes into this project. According to city records, the tax abatement for the Manhattan Plaza apartments for the year 2003 was over $9.7 million. Multiplied times 40 years (the length of the agreement) that adds up to $388 million. Add to that the HUD rent subsidies (approximately $500 per month per eligible apartment) which easily exceed $10 million a year—that adds another $400 million. Add to that $90 million dollars New York City loaned as a mortgage for construction of Manhattan Plaza ($80+million of which is still outstanding). Now we're up to around $900 million. But just to err on the conservative side, in case our estimates are off, we can safely say, the total figure is a minimum of a $500 million—a half billion dollars of taxpayers' money.

Yet Related Companies is seeking a further considerable increase of taxpayer money through Mark up to Market. We have the original Board of Estimate Contract in place until 2017, which requires no adjustments besides correcting the 168 apartments fraud (cf. 1977 Board of Estimate Resolution).

Please demand the owners give you any documents, which provide a legal basis for the separate 168 apartments and prove their compliance with the original Board of Estimate contract. If neither documents exist nor proof is forthcoming, please ask the City to take legal action against the owners. We will be happy to meet with you and we look forward to hearing from you regarding your plans and participation in this matter.

Sincerely,
Manhattan Plaza Residents Alliance
Susan Johann, President
Tony Giordano, Vice-president

SAMPLE LETTER # 2

February 17, 2005

RE: HUD Waste of Taxpayers' Monies

George W Bush
President of the United States
The White House
1600 Pennsylvania Avenue NW
Washington, D.C. 20500

Dear President Bush,

Here are facts to support your 2006 budget. It is rumored that HUD has misplaced fifty-nine billion dollars throughout the years. I do not know whether this figure is correct but this week I watched Elliott Spitzer claim he punishes government agencies who waste taxpayers monies, Hillary Clinton and Charles Schumer complain the 2006 budget demonstrates lack of compassion for the poor, and a young lady complains taxpayers are not providing enough money to help the poor. Obviously funds are not reaching the right people. Why such wastes? Is everybody doing his/her job? I have proof they are not.

I am a founder of HUD Project Section 8 housing for performing artists in New York City, called Manhattan Plaza (MP). Throughout 1976 I co-authored the rules and regulations and other documentation necessary to request taxpayers to subsidize performer artists. In March 1977 New York's Board of Estimate RESOLUTION provided for Section 8 taxpayers' subsidy for all 1669 apartments (100% of two forty-five story buildings) allocating these apartments to "at least 70% performing artists, up to 15% elderly, and up to 15% local neighbors living in substandard housing, " and no other.

The Board's RESOLUTION came with guarantees that the taxpayers' monies would be monitored and properly executed by Housing Preservation & Development (HPD), in conjunction with the MP Policy Making Management Committee (eight theatrical unions in limited partnership with the owners) of which I was a member. I am an eyewitness to the fact that those guarantees to protect taxpayers were not honored. HPD, HUD, the owners (Aquarius management), the tenant association (MPTA), the politicians and the theatrical unions (MP Policy Making Management committee), all of whom were hired or elected to preserve the RESOLUTION, did not obey the obligations outlined in the RESOLUTION. Whenever I, with others attempted to bring this issue to their attention they blocked our ability to be heard, destroying every one of our tenant rights, so determined were they to maintain their corruption. For instance, only two months after the RESOLUTION's inception, by June 1977 Housing Preservation & Development (HPD), together with the owners of MP "Aquarius Management" stole 169 apartments with no legal right, instantly preventing "at least 70% performing artists" from ever being attained at MP. As a result for the past twenty-eight years taxpayers have subsidized friends, relatives, and government staff in apartments not allocated to them.

We, the Manhattan Plaza Residents Alliance (MPRA), attempted to enlist the help from HUD, HPD, Elliot Spitzer, Hillary Clinton, Charles Schumer, Jerrold Nadler, Tom Duane, Christine Quinn, Richard Gottfried, the Mayor, the Governor, NY Borough Presidents, Comptroller Heversi and others. The Governor, the Comptroller and Elliott Spitzer told us to look elsewhere. Clinton, Schumer et al never responded. The President of Manhattan, Virginia Fields, wrote back 'you have no authorization. Work through your tenants association.'

Had Senators Clinton and Schumer et al read our documentation they would have discovered that Manhattan Plaza has nearly outlived its need for subsidy. They would have discovered that the stolen 169 apartments should act as a lien against the sale that was underway in 2004. They would have discovered there are only approximately 30 % of the tenants actively pursuing performing arts careers. They would have discovered that when the owners entered into secret sale negotiations this past year we took a survey and learned that five hundred residents were interested in purchasing their apartment as a condo non-eviction conversion, thus relieving the taxpayers. HAD Clinton and Schumer helped us they would have freed the taxpayers from this subsidy.

Imagine! Subsidized tenants who were ready, willing, and able to take responsibility off the taxpayers and no politician would help us. As if that isn't bad enough, Related Companies bought Manhattan Plaza's ongoing subsidy in 2004 without being willing to obey the Board of Estimate's Resolution, then managed to persuade HUD to give them additional subsidies, perhaps 11 million dollars more per year. At MP in a two-bedroom apartment the 169 friends pay $1750 monthly. The subsidized tenants pay $1750 for that same apartment with or without subsidy. But since the owners bought MP in '04, once the full rent is paid, taxpayers then pay an additional $1750 subsidy every month for that apartment, for a total of $3300. Multiply those monthly's by 1530 apartments.

Manhattan Plaza became a cash cow. Politicians and government workers are not doing their jobs. The owners earn larger profits than the limited profits the resolution obligates them to, all of this while betraying their mandate, misallocating apartments, and refusing to correct abuses. Who is looking out for taxpayers?

Mr. President, multiply such offenses across the United States and you will locate wastes we can ill afford. Investigate these allegations and you will open a Pandora's box of misused funds, and in so doing you will create accountability to taxpayers, a conservative thing to do. Then apply those funds to those in need, a compassionate thing to do.

I am available and prepared to provide documentation.

Sincerely,
Tony Giordano
tonygiord@aol.com

cc. Karl Rove, The White House
Kenneth M. Donohue, Sr. Inspector General HUD
Elizabeth Wright. Citizens Against Government Waste

SAMPLE LETTER # 3

May 9, 2005

President George W. Bush
1600 Pennsylvania Avenue
Washington, DC 20500

RE: Senator DeMint's RIGHT TO WORK ACT

Dear President Bush,

Thank you for the help you and Karl Rove provided regarding my HUD allegations last month. I enclose a copy of the action the Inspector General is taking (cf. Inspector General).

As I sign the petition for the Senator's Right to Work ACT today I want to share with you and Senator DeMint corruptions within our government that might stand in its way.

I am a freelance Theatre Director. For ten years I was Executive Vice President of the Society of Stage Directors and Choreographers (SSDC), registered with the Department of Labor as a national labor union. From 1988 to 1991 I was the union's lead negotiator over the Minimum Basic Agreement (MBA) opposite the League of Resident Theatres (LORT). A major stumbling block in those negotiations, which led to a near strike, involved artistic directors of LORT theatres who refused to pay assessments for their work when they directed plays within their own theatres. They argued that artistic directors were managers and when they directed a play in their theatre their directing work was also managerial. Therefore they could not obey labor rules or pay labor assessments.

Functioning under a misapprehension that SSDC was a legitimate labor union, which we had been assured of for years by the Labor Department, I and my committee insisted the SSDC always had the motto: All for One/One for All. We insisted that all directors performed the duty of directing in the same way. That nothing artistic directors did in rehearsals to bring a show together was different from the way any freelance director did and therefore they should pay the same assessments as every other director. When we were unable to dispel their desire to be exempt from assessments we brought this matter to the National Labor Relations Board (NLRB).

The NLRB then made a Determination that these directors did not have to pay assessments to direct plays, and that they could retain full membership in the SSDC, including positions on the SSDC board of directors, thus making decisions affecting the work and assessments of all other directors. Ever since, these directors have a separate "Memorandum of Understanding" in perpetuity, which provides the above rights, none of which were granted to any other director.

Because of the NLRB's shocking determination to provide separate rights for directing a play I became curious and investigated the LABOR ACT and discovered that the NLRB's Determination was an egregious misuse of the LABOR ACT. They were partially correct because I discovered for the first time that there are six categories of workers in America who are not permitted to form Labor unions under the auspices of the Department of Labor: farmers, armed forces, railroad workers, supervisors, independent contractors and managers so it was correct to determine that because these directors fit the categories of workers outside the purview of labor unions, they need not pay assessments to a labor union. But why was the Department of Labor agreeing to make a Determination on behalf of workers outside their purview. And I could not help but wonder how the SSDC ever became a labor union for directors under the protection of the Department of Labor and why this Labor Department was making such a strange Determination to provide separate rights for directing a play where some directors must obey labor rules, but others not.

None of this made any sense. Especially since the Labor ACT also insists that while these six categories of workers may form other kinds of unions, they cannot be Labor unions or protected by the Department of Labor. The Department of Labor has no purview or right to protect non-labor unions. The Act also reveals that non labor unions cannot force any individual worker to join its membership, in contrast to Labor Unions who maintain a protected monopoly by the Department of Labor. Further, any single worker within these six categories has the freedom from all labor unions and the right to refuse membership in non-labor unions. Simply stated, these workers HAVE THE RIGHT TO WORK. By determining on behalf of these directors to not pay assessments the NLRB was acting outside its purview and operating a labor agency on behalf of managers.

Joined by three other directors I applied for a personal hearing with the New York National Relations Board, and after an enormous and significant effort to gain their attention they finally saw us. We made our case very clearly that directors belonged to three of the six categories of workers outside the purview of the LABOR ACT: independent contractors, supervisors, and managers. We argued that as long as the NLRB decided to make this Determination on behalf of the directors referred to in the Memorandum of Understanding they had to extend its terms to every director within the SSDC. And we concluded if they continued to discriminate against other directors in their determination to exempt some directors from assessments who they view as managers, the NLRB was implicitly making an illegal determination that all other directors were labor.

So we demonstrated that every director is an arm of management; showed documentation where directing contracts provide property rights (directors own their work, which cannot be used without payment). We explained how directors hire and fire (duties of managers) and how they advice producers to hire and fire (duties of supervisors as defined within the Labor Act). That it did not matter whether the director was also an artistic director because when the artistic director directed a play in his or her theatre he or she still behaved exactly the same as any director who was not also an artistic director. That freelance directors often owned the play itself and were obligated to be its caretaker throughout its history, adding responsibilities larger than those of artistic directors. How could a director who owned the play abandon their production during some strike from their labor union?

At a meeting in their New York office NLRB top Executive Daniel Silverman told us that we were right about all of this and as such we held the hammer. But if we forced him to use that hammer we would topple unions all across America. He argued that closing down a union was bad for our industry and the NLRB was not in the business of closing unions.

We replied that the moment the NLRB made the determination that some directors were not obligated to labor assessments we investigated and discovered that the Society of Stage Directors and Choreographers was illegitimately created and condoned under the faulty auspices of the Department of Labor. And that was not our fault. We felt the Department of Labor had the obligation to stop the creation of this labor union based solely on the supervisory nature of directors' work, and it failed to do so. Time had now arrived for correction, especially in view of the NLRB's determination to excuse some directors from assessments, thus exacerbating discrimination. Regarding the assertion this was bad for the industry we argued that directors still had the option to become a Guild, but without monopolies and protections provided by the Department of Labor. That nothing could be worse for the industry than rules inappropriately defining directors as labor.

We insisted that NLRB use the hammer they claimed we held. They agreed to do so.

Several weeks later we received a letter from the NLRB that we had no Standing to create a Unit Clarification. We were too small a group to be a Unit, and only a Unit could affect change. They dropped the case. Clearly they never intended to fulfill their promise.

We then realized the size and scope of this governmental corruption: that the NLRB disobeyed the Labor ACT when it created the illegitimate labor union (SSDC) for managers, supervisors, and independent contractors and no matter how hard we would try to correct the problem the NLRB would rather sustain ongoing wrongs than ever admit their original fault. We realized that they made a determination for the special group in the Memorandum of Understanding when by law they should have simply admitted that making any determination on behalf of Managers, etc was outside their purview.

And we realized that the very notion that we had no Standing, when we had proven to them that we were managers, supervisors and independent contractors, meant they were willing to continue to disobey the Labor ACT which provided independence to our three categories of work. By treating us as laborers they were forcing us to remain in an illegitimate labor union, without equal rights to other directors, and totally preventing us from the rights the Labor ACT had provided for us. So we were to remain indentured servants! We appealed but the Washington NLRB office supported the New York office.

I then resigned my membership in the SSDC based on the supervisory nature of my work and because my new knowledge made it impossible for me to sit passively and watch the SSDC force new directors into its illegitimate union. With my resignation I instantly went from being the union's most contracted director, who received more yearly contracts across America than any other member (which is why I had been elected to become the lead negotiator) to not working at all within that jurisdiction. The artistic directors, who now sit as members of the Board of Directors at the SSDC, and their Managing Directors from the LORT theatres, used their joint powers to blackball me from working as a director and I had no government agency to complain to.

During that period of time SSDC stole my health benefit of $3000.00 due to me from the one and only time I had ever used my medical coverage because I was attempting to cure sinus problems. They insisted I had no coverage. I wrote to the Pension and Welfare Trustees and submitted proof that I had coverage. The Trustees guaranteed they would investigate. Then they wrote and insisted I was not covered, which was a lie. Five of the Trustees who promised to investigate had been involved in the dispute over the Memorandum of Understanding, including the two attorneys for the SSDC and the LORT theatres. When I complained to the Department of Labor they informed me they do not interfere or dispute Trustees over union rules. Etc.

Sorry to say there is more. My career began in 1968 (cf. Curriculum Vitae) and is a classic example that the legislators who created the Labor Act in the 1930's to protect us from Labor unions were correct. My journey to direct plays across America has moved me to and fro and could never have been limited to one jurisdiction, or one union. But instead of protection I was forced from the very beginning into Actors Equity Association union (AEA). I paid dues and assessments for eight years to direct plays, while producers paid my pension and welfare to AEA. In 1976 the SSDC was formed under the auspices of the Department of Labor and I was forced to move out of AEA, where I had worked under directing contracts for eight years and into the Society of Directors and Choreographers (SSDC). During the next fifteen years I worked consistently through SSDC, but also had to join The Director's Guild of America (DGA), another Labor union when I directed Television, or when I went to direct three shows in Canadian theatre and had to go through New York's Actors Equity Association in order to join Canadian Actors Equity.

When my time to receive pension payments was approaching I discovered that Actors Equity Association threw away my entire pension of eight years. They claim I needed ten years to vest. When I pointed out that I was unable to continue to work in their union as a director for the ninth and tenth year once they no longer covered directors they insisted that was not their fault. When I pointed out that I had three added years through Canadian Actors Equity for a total of eleven years, they stated that they stopped having reciprocal pension relationships with Canada (prior to the three shows I directed under their joint auspices). When I explained to them that they should have moved my pension fund to the SSDC when the SSDC took over jurisdiction of directors under the auspices of the Department of Labor they told me to take a hike. I contacted the Department of Labor's Pension department, asked them to intercede. I asked them to show me any legitimacy that Actors Equity ever had the right to cover directors, but the Labor Department refused to investigate.

The Directors Guild of America also has divided my pension in such a way as to virtually erase its values because I do not have the ten years they require to vest. But I was never primarily a television director and though I actually directed many shows these did not constitute ten years for vesting. And of course Canadian Equity has thrown away payments meant for me for the same reason. In each of these pension circumstances these unions are creating rules of work which might more appropriately involve a laborer or someone who daily punches into a factory. Once the Department of Labor accepts and sanctions the creation of these unions they subsequently permit the unions to create pension rules for laborers. I wrote and called many times to the Department of Labor's Pension and Welfare division but they refused to investigate, also claiming they never interfere with Trustees of Unions and their rules, and eventually discontinued accepting my calls.

Then I wrote to Senator Hillary Clinton and submitted elaborate documentation. This was several years ago. I followed with numerous phone calls and have never received any response, including even a postcard of acknowledgment. It is interesting now for me to receive from Senator DeMint a petition to sign by me to Senator Clinton in order for her to provide the Right to Work. Who are we kidding?

In the past several years I have cleverly found alternate ways to create, though not yet to make a living. I have written a screenplay called BROOKLYN ODYSSEY and hope to make a film if and when money is available. It will be a film that encourages the value of great education. I traveled to Belgium to attain the rights so that I could adapt a Dutch musical into English, called SACCO and VANZETTI, which I now call THE AMERICAN DREAM and which demonstrates a need for us to fulfill our dream, yet unrealized. And last year at this time I traveled with a general license from the Treasury Department to Havana, Cuba to finish a musical I wrote called HAVANA CARNAVAL.

I am grateful that I was forced to work overseas because it demonstrates all too clearly what an independent contractor I am. The Department of Labor, and the National Relations Board should make restitution to me for the headaches and the monies I lost in the process of being covered illegitimately by unions who provided nothing more than trouble to my career. If possible please help to investigate this issue on my behalf, for every time I seek an attorney I am informed their law firms have a conflict of interest. On one occasion an attorney wondered where the pot of gold was and how she could make a killing when the money involved seemed so insignificant. She was right about the money, but that is why our government should not cheat a worker like myself out of his insignificant sums.

At this time, because the SSDC, the DGA, the AEA continue to be sponsored as a labor union with monopoly powers to force membership by the Department of Labor I live in a country that makes it nearly impossible for me to make a living. And considering the success of my freelance career I am appalled that preventing me from working, stealing my benefits and trying to force me to be a laborer, could possibly be good for me or my industry. Yet every time I do now work in America I have to search to find one of the rare producers who accept a contract with me, outside the purview of these unions. This is a very difficult and costly chore I assure you! Most producers are afraid of confronting these unions and would rather not be bothered to enter into a contractual dispute. However, when there is a National Right to Work Act these producers will be thrilled to be free of the nonsense of unions. I have overwhelming documentation for everything I have told you in this letter. I will make that documentation and myself available to Senator DeMint, or whomever you choose.

Mr. President, you are my favorite person in the world today. I view you as the brightest man alive because I define intelligence as the ability to change the world. And you are doing just that despite the many people trying to block you from becoming a great president. But I feel that you place too much value and waste too much energy in making peace with your congressional enemies. Nothing will ever cause them to cooperate with you or any other Republican in the White House. They have lost their cool.

Please forgive my personal intrusion as I plead with you to dedicate the remainder of your valued Presidency to cleaning up our government in matters similar to this Right to Work and the housing fraud I earlier wrote about, which I view as economic terrorism. Please do for our country what no one else is capable of doing at present. And since you will not be running for a third term what a great opportunity lies before you. Force our government to clean up its ongoing wrongs.

But most especially, when Senator DeMint creates this Right to Work Act be aware that there are those in government who will defy it on a daily basis and smother its very existence. The creation of a new ACT is not sufficient. The LABOR ACT as I outlined above failed me because it was not properly monitored, not because it was incorrectly legislated. The same is true of the waste of taxpayers' monies in HUD. The Board of Estimate Resolution, which created Section 8 subsidy for Manhattan Plaza was brilliantly legislated. But the government agencies obligated to monitor it, dug into it as if it was a cash cow.

Once created, The Right to Work ACT must be guarded daily, evaluated often to be certain it has not veered from its intentions, and reported to the President and the Congress yearly. It must be protected from those in government whose refusal to execute such an ACT, I am sorry to prophesize, will be a certainty. Appoint a Czar to monitor all the ACTS if need be!

President George W Bush, I give you my greatest respect, support, love and prayers and thank God for your Presidency.

Tony Giordano
www.tonygiordano.us
cc. James DeMint, Karl Rove

SAMPLE LETTER # 4

September 11, 2008

President George W. Bush
The White House
Washington, D.C. 20502
Steve Preston, Secretary, HUD, &
Kenneth Donohue, Insp. Gen, HUD
U.S. Department of HUD
451 7th St., S.W.
Washington D.C. 20410

RE: HJ-05-1047
FIIG47481BP (tracking)

Dear President Bush and Messrs Preston & Donohue,

For years I pursued investigations regarding misuse of taxpayers monies at HUD's Section 8 Manhattan Plaza housing for Performing Artists in New York City where I live and am a founder. Finally I submitted one of my complaints to you, Mr. President, in my letter dated February 21, 2005 and you graciously forwarded it to the Inspector General.

The Office of Inspector General then contacted me and asked that I submit any further documentation, which I did, and told me to wait until contacted. Three and a half years later I have now received their answer, which is a complete and insulting avoidance of every one of my allegations, an obvious sham, consistent with the previous years of obvious shams, in which HUD, HPD and now the Inspector General simply refuse to answer the allegations in my complaints. I have experienced this idiotic behavior for the past thirty years and that is long enough.

I once again turn to you, Mr. President, and Messrs Preston and Donoghue to appoint someone with a lack of conflict of interest to answer my allegations, probably outside the jurisdiction of the OIG. As a citizen I have this right. Mr. Donoghue, OIG'S independent status cannot possibly permit OIG an opportunity of falsification, which has just been exposed by your response to my complaint. I am enclosing in each of your envelopes total and complete documentation between OIG and myself. Without much effort you will see clearly OIG's refusal to address the allegations. But please read through the remainder of this letter because I have unveiled some things to help us see inexcusable waste of taxpayers' monies, and violation of tenants' rights.

To refresh the topic, I am one of the founders of Manhattan Plaza who began the task of writing the regulations that led to this subsidy for performing artists in 1975. About ten of us met weekly for approximately fifteen months to accomplish a task that had no precedence other than the obligation to obey the rules of federal housing. One of these rules required that this housing complex include *at least* 70% performing artists to maintain the subsidy and Manhattan Plaza's status as HUD housing for Performing Artists. Another rule was that all 100% of the apartments were section 8. Each of the three varieties of apartments, studio, one or two bedrooms, had only one ceiling price. Tenants would pay 30% of their income up to the full price. The apartments were to be divided according to a breakdown of *at least* 70% performing artists, up to 15% of senior citizens, and up to 15% of local residents in substandard housing. The entire subsidy included only those three categories of applicants, no others. Because income was an issue the federal regulation added the notion that up to 10% of the tenants had the right to earn enough money to pay the ceiling rent and still be considered subsidized tenants because the incomes from their careers varied year to year, and since every apartment was section 8 the tenant who paid ceiling price in one year who needed subsidy in a following year had that subsidy sitting and waiting on his or her behalf.

We pursued our tasks until we completed the paperwork that assured the taxpayers they're monies would be monitored and protected. As a result we received the subsidy in March 1977. As soon as we began to provide housing to the constituents, Laila Long of Housing Preservation and Development along with Rodney Kirk, the manager of Manhattan Plaza came to our committee in June 1977, just two months into the subsidy, to inform us that the federal government told them to re-allocate 10% (167 apartments) outside the rules and regulations of the Board of Estimate's Determination, into a fourth category of tenants, at the discretion of the owners.

At this point Laila Long moved into a two-bedroom apartment and Rodney Kirk and his owners, Irv Fisher and Richard Ravitch, began to provide apartments to friends, relatives, and members of the government. This very point in time, June 1977, began the core of a problem that exists to this day:

i.e. the artists sought the subsidy; the taxpayers provided it; but the owners in conjunction with the government lied to get more of the share than was their right. And since this lie was made both by the owners, and a leading dignitary in a government position, then throughout the past thirty years it has been impossible to restore the misallocated apartments, because HPD and HUD have protected the owners of Manhattan Plaza through virtually every complaint made by tenants.

From June 1977 the owners, in conjunction with HPD and HUD created a coalition to block anyone from revealing this lie eventually including the tenant' association, and the policy committee members who supposedly represent the artists. Tenants who live in Manhattan Plaza have had most of their rights taken away, despite the fact it was artists who sought the subsidy and taxpayers who provided it.

I have spent the past thirty years trying to restore misallocation of those apartments, instigate tenants' rights, in particular a right of first refusal to purchase (due to a condo conversion vote that took place), and an ongoing very serious issue with deductions for professional expenses that demonstrates total discrimination by the owners and the government. But in every single document of evidence and proof I have ever submitted HPD and HUD has done what the Inspector General just did, avoid the complaint totally, never investigating into the issue for the truth. Regarding the discrimination issue in professional expenses I hired a law firm, Shearman and Sterling and they submitted to HUD a detailed, clear and elaborate presentation of the issue only to receive a response in two paragraphs that basically concluded, "we don't agree."

During the past thirty years Ms Long, Mr. Kirk and all the government agents who had been hired at HPD and HUD not only closed their eyes to the misallocation of the apartments, they created a baffle to confuse the issue. Their baffle has cost taxpayers more money than necessary to run the building and prevented constituents who deserved these apartments from occupancy. Ms Long and Mr. Kirk insisted that a fourth category of tenants were meant to be included in the Board of Estimate Determination. So they fabricated that this fourth category was what was intended when the Determination permitted up to 10% of the tenants to be able to pay fair market. In other words they simply took the phrase up to 10%, regarding the right to stay as subsidized tenants despite high income, and chose to interpret that it meant there was a separate category of tenant up to 10%.

But since all 100% apartments were section 8, which was very clear in all documentation and only three categories fit into that 100%, they then listed the 10% as Mitchell Lama apartments. They did this while knowing full well that all 100% were section 8. At first they allowed their Mitchell Lama tenants to slide down into Section 8, which was easy enough to do since section 8 covered every apartment. Then eventually when we continued to rail against their dirty deed they claimed these Mitchell Lama tenants would remain separate from section 8. Regardless of what they did, they clearly refused to restore those apartments to 100% Section 8, permanently preventing justified constituents from a right to occupy those apartments, and creating a coalition that has prevented any tenant who seeks rights from receiving them. Try sending a complaint to HPD or HUD or the Tenant's Association, the Policy Committee, the manager, Irv Fisher, etc. and watch the clock ticking while you wait for an answer, which never, ever arrives. So professional expenses are never re-opened to correct discrimination. So a tenant's association that is controlled by management is permitted to shout and scream at people and when you remind everyone that Roberts Rules of Order were obligated in the by-Laws but never incorporated at the meetings no one answers and the association is left free to follow the dictates of management.

Every effort I made to correct these matters hit brick walls, not because anyone disagreed but because every one at HUD and HPD who I asked to investigate managed to avoid answering the issue, either by sending no response, or by an inane response that did not address the issue as in the case of OIG's recent response. I have the documentation to prove this. And the tenant association prior to the present one has their documentation as well, which also proves how impossible it is here to receive one's rights. But the refusal to answer our complaints has begun to ring loud and clear: THEY ARE GUILTY. THEY KNOW IT. If they enter into investigation and try to deny the evidence they will be revealed, so they avoid investigating at all costs, hoping it will wash away.

Despite the great things about living here Manhattan Plaza has become a cash cow, a government waste, a total injustice to taxpayers and a building that represses tenants by preventing them from their tenant rights. But of course, if no one will investigate then everyone can assume whatever he or she wishes. I provide the complaints. I demand the investigation.

A major exception was Ruth Lerner, who at the time was the HPD official representative of this project and who loudly insisted that the 167 apartments in question belonged to the 100% Section 8 apartments, and only to constituents established and defined in the Board of Estimate Determination. She tried to prevent Irv Fisher from proceeding to misallocate those apartments. Furthermore, she insisted that every rightful constituent who was denied one of those misappropriated 167 apartments could sue since they had the sole right to the apartments. Yet the lie of Laila Long and Rodney Kirk prevailed and HPD and HUD proved there are none so blind as those who refuse to see.

Mr. President, soon after you connected me to OIG in 2005, OIG informed me they might appoint a special prosecutor to avoid a conflict of interest since my complaint involves HPD and HUD. I was told that each of my allegations would be fully investigated. With relief, I thought, "Finally, someone cares about taxpayers." On the contrary, when last month, I finally called OIG I discovered that the case closed a year ago. OIG had never bothered to send me a notice. So I requested a FOIA and what I read last week reveals that instead of investigating my allegations, as promised, OIG failed to investigate even one single allegation. Also, OIG asked Deborah Van Amerongen, Director, New York Housing Division, 2AHMLA to investigate and the letterhead of her report lists her as working for HUD.

Unless OIG failed to give Ms Amerongen my letters and documents, which could explain her inadequate and skimpy report, she functioned with a total conflict of interest. If you first read my allegations, then read Ms Amerongen's report to OIG you will have little doubt that HUD knows all too well how guilty they are over this matter and that is why they choose to avoid investigating it.

Ms Amerongen asked Hector Pinero, a manager today of Related Co, to provide a response, except it was to her own invented version, not mine, against Related Co.'s present managerial operation, which has only existed for several years. Neither Mr. Pinero nor Related Co. were involved in this housing complex during the issues of my complaint, the first twenty-five years.

The only reference in my complaint that involves Related Co was that prior to their purchase of Manhattan Plaza four or five years ago 520 tenants (over 15%) signed statements that they wished for a condo, non-eviction conversion and this would obviously relieve the taxpayers. But as soon as the tenant vote was completed the rights of the tenants were smothered and their desire to take responsibility away from the taxpayers blocked, collectively by HPD, HUD, Aquarius Management, Related Company, the tenant's association and the Policy Committee. At no point were the tenants who desired this condo conversion permitted at place at the table of the negotiations. The President of the Tenant association and the members of the Policy Committee even bragged openly how they aiding Aquarius in selling and Related Co. in purchasing the complex, helping Related in the process to receive quite a bit of additional subsidy. So rather than freeing taxpayers from this financial obligation they managed to increase the burden on the taxpayer, considerably.

However, though this was my only real reference in my complaint against Related Ms Van Amerongen failed to address it in any case, using as I stated earlier, her own scenario. Among all the other complaints she bypassed she demonstrated no interest in my complaint about tenant's rights, a condo conversion, prevention to negotiate, and the unified bond that had been created against the tenants by all of the groups listed above, and no interest in the 167 apartments.

The owners were free to sell Manhattan Plaza as if they had paid the bills almost as if it was there gift to performing arts, rejecting thirty years of funds from taxpayers who provided all the money and who are responsible for the success of this complex, as well as the contribution the artists made by seeking the subsidy, which saved the owners from near catastrophe. For in the early days when the owners knew they were not going to be able to rent in hell's kitchen they asked artists to save their asses and we did. But once accomplished the tenants and the taxpayers have been stepped over in significant ways. Read HUD documents about tenants rights and you find virtually none of them available at Manhattan Plaza.

Both set of owners, Aquarius and Related, have touted Manhattan Plaza as the miracle on 42nd Street but from the very beginning, when Laila Long and Rodney Kirk lied and squirreled 167 apartments, performing artists who deserved those apartments were cut out, the Board of Estimate's Determination which commanded *at least* 70% performing artists was vitiated instantly, and a lien should have been placed upon the complex until these apartments and the performing artists percentage was restored.

So, the lien, in conjunction with the government's refusal to provide tenants with a right of first refusal to purchase should have blocked Related Co. from its purchase, but of course who in government was obeying the rules of HUD?

As I mentioned several times Ms. Long and Rodney Kirk claimed the 167 apartments were never meant to be section 8. So I provided to OIG documentation to prove that 100% of the apartments were meant to be section 8. Then they claimed the 167 apartments were Mitchell Lama, but my documentation proves that claim to also be false.

Aquarius management sold the 1700 apartment complex to Related Co. for only One Hundred and Fifty Million Dollars ($150,000,000.00). Related used the illegitimate167, which were never re-allocated to the 100% section 8 Determination, to match the rents in the neighborhood, into Blue contracts. Then they managed to get HUD to give them almost double the former subsidy on every other apartment to match the raised rents from the 167 blue contracts. A cash cow! And the taxpayers are none the wiser. With the help of the government they legitimized a category of illegitimate 167 apartments in order to force the taxpayers to provide a mechanism for twice as much subsidy.

First, the tenants lost their right to purchase this complex for $150,000,000; then taxpayers were forced to provide more subsidy without agreement, and Related Co. and Aquarius management fell into a gold mine.

Here is how it works, and forgive my figures, for they are approximates. A two-bedroom apartment for section 8 tenants has a ceiling on it of $2200.00. That same apartment for the non-section 8 apartments is $3400.00 monthly. These tenants pay the entire $3400.00. The section 8 tenant pays only 30% of their income for that apartment, but never more than its ceiling of $2200.00. The 30% rent, in some cases, can be $500.00 or even less, at which point the taxpayers would then have to subsidize $1700.00 per month for that section 8 tenant who only pays $500. But, now with the additional subsidies, $1200.00 per month is further added to match the new ceiling paid by the Blue contracts. In this case, the taxpayer is providing $2900.00 per month for one tenant, times twelve months, which comes to $34.800.00 per year, per one tenant. And there are 1700 apartments in this complex. The taxpayers provide these monies, every day. Taxpayers who work, pay rent, pay their mortgages, pay their costs of living are contributing overwhelming monies per apartment to people like themselves, except the money moves fast into the hands of Related Co. and the sweet retirement deals of Aquarius. One middle manager is about to retire now to a $3,000,000 retirement package. And this is subsidized housing. If the tenants had acquired the condo conversion such excess would not have occur.

With facts like these it is no wonder HUD refuses to investigate. I repeat, Ms Amerongen authored a complaint against Related Co as if I had made the complaint then sought a response from Hector Pinero. Then after Mr. Pinero answered her complaint Ms Amerongen concluded "we feel comfortable with the position the subject project's owner (i.e. Pinero) has taken with respect to the overall integrity and professionalism of the Aquarius Management Corp. The likelihood that the allegations in question are true is, in our estimate, remote at best."

Ms Amerongen used her own fantasy to conclude "the likelihood the allegations in question are true is, in our estimate, remote at best." But my complaint has no need for her estimation since I am eyewitness to all of my allegations and my evidence factually corroborates my allegations.

As an example, in my papers to OIG I made the claim, as I mentioned above, that within the first two months of the subsidy (June 1977), Laila Long of HPD and Rodney Kirk of Aquarius Management claimed the government sent them to extract 167 apartments for personal use by the owners. Nine years later we investigated and discovered there never had been any government who sent them to re-allocate these apartments. They simply lied. My corroborating evidence is a copy of Ms Long's "Memo to files" that is virtually a confession because it states that she and Rodney Kirk made that decision in her office alone and in a single afternoon. No mention is made of any federal government involved in their dirty deed. The owners knew of this falsehood, and HPD and HUD were informed about it on numerous occasions. Before Related Co. sought to purchase Manhattan Plaza there was nearly twenty-five years to make the correction.

In HUD housing, do the tenants not have the first refusal right to negotiate for purchase and if yes, why were the tenants at Manhattan Plaza prevented from doing so? Do the taxpayers have a right to expect that their monies be applied to all 100% of the apartments as they originally agreed to as defined in their agreement with the Board of Estimate Determination, rather than allowing HUD, HPD, and the owners to alter the agreement without an agreement with taxpayers, while pushing the artists aside who deserved to live in these apartments? Do taxpayers have a right to insist that a lien should exist on a building that failed to maintain Board of Estimate's Determination, which is basically the two part agreement between the taxpayers and those who chose to use their money. The only other contact I had with Related Co. occurred prior to their purchase. I submitted to Steve Ross of Related Co., all of this data in this letter and suggested the misallocated apartments should be viewed as a lien, so none of this should come to them today as a surprise.

Mr. President, despite your enormous responsibilities, and Messrs. Preston and Donoghue with your huge agencies I am asking as one of the citizens who wrote documentation to create Manhattan Plaza and request taxpayers to spend their money on this project, to join me in my personal sense of responsibility to fully investigate my claim that our government and the owners of Manhattan Plaza have created ongoing wrongs in this subsidy and I think your attention to this matter is essential.

So, with your powerful positions plus my willingness as an unpaid citizen who has taken the time to provide the evidence, investigate.

Here's how. I believe the tenants' right of first refusal to negotiate for a condo non eviction complex should be provided, now, because it was denied when it shouldn't have been, and purchased at the price Related Co. paid four years ago, $150,000,000, which will then function to restore the problem of the other 167 apartments. I will make myself available to you but please do not request as OIG did in 2005 that I sit quietly by and keep silent. I wasted over three years of this serious matter trusting in OIG. In the meantime, I am submitting to you Mr. President, and you Mr. Preston and Mr. Donoghue, all the documentation I submitted previously to OIG. Please, investigate!

Perhaps each of you should appoint three separate investigators and compare their reports, and maybe one of them should be from the Department of Justice.

Sincerely,
Tony Giordano
www.tonygiordano.us
1 212 947 0443
tonygiord@aol.com
c.c. Citizens Against Government Waste, Tom Schatz